IDENTITY REVOLUTION

"Why Identity in Christ Changes Everything"

Dr. Jean Héder Petit-Frère

Published by:
Kingdom Records Unlimited

ISBN: 978-1-971611-06-8

Printed in the United States of America

www.jhpetitfrere.com

Dedication

I dedicate this to every believer who has loved God sincerely, yet lived beneath the reality of who they truly are.

I am writing to the sons and daughters who have served faithfully but are now ready to stand confidently.

I am writing to those who are weary of performance and hungry for truth. May this book mark the moment when identity is no longer rehearsed, but fully embraced.

And to my family, who have walked with me through revelation, growth, tension, and grace, thank you for allowing truth to mature in our lives before it reached these pages.

This revolution begins within.

ACKNOWLEDGMENTS

No work of this kind is ever written in a vacuum.

The message of this book was molded not only in study, prayer, and years of ministry, but also in community, in relationships that challenged, supported, corrected, and carried me through the seasons of growth.

I am grateful to those who have let me test, refine, and live the truth before it was published. Your faithfulness, your inquiries, and your endurance have added to the lucidity of these pages.

To my family, who have walked with me through seasons of revelation and responsibility, thank you for your patience, your sacrifices, and your unfailing support. This work reflects the pieces of our common path; this book is as much yours as it is mine.

To every believer, leader, and student of the Kingdom who has sat under this teaching, grappled with its consequences, and chosen to develop rather than retreat.

Finally, all praise is due to God, the source of life, truth, and revelation. Without Him, there is no message, no transformation, and no purpose in writing.

May this work serve as a tool to inform, to establish identity, and to strengthen individuals who read it.

Author's Note

This book was not written to inspire emotion. It was written to correct the perspective.

For years, I have observed sincere believers who love God deeply, yet struggle internally with insecurity, performance, fear, and instability. This is not due to a lack of devotion, but rather a lack of clarity.

The crisis in the Church is not primarily moral. It is not intellectual. It is not even cultural. It is not even spiritual. It is an identity crisis.

Many understand forgiveness, but have not embraced new creation. Many believe in Christ but have not learned to live in that union. Many pray, serve, and strive, yet remain uncertain of who they are before God.

Identity Revolution is an invitation to settle that question.

This book does not attack the Church. It calls her higher. It does not introduce novelty; it restores emphasis. It does not offer spiritual techniques; it realigns foundations.

If at any point the pages confront you, let them. If they unsettle assumptions, allow it. Revolutions always begin by dismantling what is unstable.

Read slowly. Reflect deeply. And most importantly, allow the Holy Spirit to anchor truth beyond theory.

Identity must move from concept to conviction. That is the journey ahead.

Dr. Jean Héder Petit-Frère

Preface

The Crisis Beneath the Surface

There is a difference between believing in Christ and living from Him. Across churches, conferences, and leadership circles, I have witnessed a recurring pattern: believers who are passionate yet uncertain, gifted yet insecure, and committed yet exhausted. The issue is rarely devotion. It is identity.

When identity is unclear, effort increases. When identity is unstable, striving multiplies. Performance takes the place of tranquility when identity is unresolved. The gospel does not merely forgive sin. It establishes identity.

It does not simply remove guilt. It recreates the believer. It does not recruit servants. It restores sons.

This book exists because the Church does not need more activity. It needs clarity. It does not need louder voices. It needs deeper roots. An identity settled in Christ produces:

rest without passivity

- authority without arrogance
- humility without insecurity
- obedience without fear

Until identity is established, growth remains fragile. This is not a call to self-discovery. It is a call to Christ-centered clarity. And clarity changes everything.

Contents

Introduction

Why Identity Changes Everything

Every struggle traces back to a question of identity. Fear, striving, insecurity, comparison, exhaustion, pride, and hesitation are symptoms. Beneath them lies a deeper issue: misunderstanding who we are in Christ.

From the beginning, humanity's crisis began with a distorted question: *"Did God really say?"*

That question was not about information. It was about identity.

When identity becomes unclear, behavior becomes unstable. The gospel answers the identity question definitively:

- You are in Christ.
- Christ lives in you.
- You are a new creation.
- You are righteous by gift.
- You are adopted as a son.
- You are an heir, not an employee.

These are not motivational slogans. They are legal realities.

Yet many believers live as though they remain distant from God, working toward acceptance rather than from it.

This book invites you to reconsider everything you thought you understood about the Christian life, not to complicate it, but to simplify it.

You were never meant to strive toward identity. You were meant to live from it. This is the revolution.

How To Use This Book

This book is designed for reflection and integration.

You may:

- Read one chapter at a time and meditate slowly.
- Use it in a leadership or discipleship setting.
- Pair it later with the companion workbook for deeper personal application.

Do not rush through it. Revolutions are not sparked by speed; they are sustained by conviction.

Allow each chapter to confront, clarify, and settle what has remained uncertain.

Chapter 1: You Cannot Feel Spiritual Reality

Revelation, Not Emotion, Is the Doorway into Truth

One of the most damaging assumptions in modern Christianity is the belief that feelings are reliable interpreters of spiritual truth. This assumption is usually unstated, yet it quietly governs how many believers understand salvation, righteousness, prayer, and even God Himself.

It also quietly shapes how you measure progress. If you feel strong, you assume you are doing well. If you feel weak, you assume you are failing. That is not discernment. That is emotional measurement.

Statements like *"I don't feel saved,"* *"I don't feel close to God,"* *"I don't feel righteous,"* or *"I don't feel anointed"* are often treated as honest spiritual assessments. They are honest emotionally, but they are not accurate spiritually.

Those statements describe experience, not position. They describe mood, not covenant reality.

Spiritual reality does not submit itself to emotional verification. If it did, truth would shift hourly. The kingdom would become unstable, and identity would be a moving target.

You cannot know your spirit through feelings, just as you cannot know your appearance through intuition. A person may feel tall or short, attractive or unattractive, strong or weak, but none of those feelings alter objective reality. Reality exists independently of how it is perceived.

In the same way, what occurred when you were born again did not take place in your emotional realm. It did not take place in your personality. It did not even take place in your conscious mind. It took place in your spirit, a realm that feelings cannot directly access.

This is why spiritual growth often feels slower than spiritual change. Change can be immediate in your spirit, while your emotions and mind may take time to catch up.

This is why Scripture never commands believers to feel saved. They are never instructed to feel righteous. It never tells them to feel holy or feel accepted.

Instead, Scripture treats salvation as an accomplished fact, not a daily emotional achievement. It consistently uses language such as *"know," "reckon," "consider," "believe,"* and *"be persuaded."* These are not emotional words. They are cognitive and revelatory words.

They point to a different kind of knowing, one that is built on God's testimony, not your internal atmosphere.

Emotions Respond; They Do Not Discover

Emotions should not guide the Christian life. Emotions are responders; they are not discoverers. They react to what the mind believes to be true.

This is why you can feel peace when you believe you are safe and feel panic when you believe you are threatened, even if nothing external changes. Emotion follows interpretation.

This explains a paradox many sincere believers experience: *"I know what the Bible says, but I don't feel like it's true."*

That tension does not mean the Bible is wrong. It means emotions are being asked to do a job they were never designed to do.

You were never created to verify the Word through sensation. You were created to align with the Word through faith.

The Limits of Feelings

Feelings are real, but they are not authoritative. They are shaped by memory, trauma, habit, chemistry, environment, fatigue, and expectation. Two people can experience the same event and feel entirely different emotions, yet the event itself remains unchanged.

This is why you can wake up feeling condemned with no new sin or feel distant with no new separation. The emotion may be real, but the conclusion is false.

If feelings were reliable guides to truth, faith would be unnecessary. Scripture introduces faith precisely because reality often precedes experience.

Faith is not fantasy. Faith is agreement with God's reality before your emotions have caught up to it.

Paul does not say, *"You will feel dead to sin."* He says, *"Consider yourselves dead to sin."* He does not say, *"You will feel righteous."* He says, *"You have been made righteous."* He does not say, *"You will feel seated with Christ."* He says, *"You are seated with Him."*

These are identity statements. They are declarations of position. They are not waiting for emotional confirmation to become true.

Faith is not a denial of emotion; it is a refusal to enthrone it.

Faith does not pretend you feel strong. Faith refuses to let weakness define the truth.

When believers allow feelings to define truth, identity becomes unstable. One day, they feel confident; the next day, condemned. One day, they feel bold in prayer; the next day, hesitant. God appears close one moment and distant the next, not because God has changed, but because perception has. This produces a fragile Christianity, one that rises and falls with emotional weather.

It also produces spiritual exhaustion, because you are constantly trying to "get back" to a feeling instead of standing in what is already true.

Why the New Covenant Requires a Different Way of Knowing

Under the Old Covenant, the relationship with God was mediated externally, through priests, sacrifices, laws, and rituals. Under the New Covenant, God relocated. He transitioned from being with His people to being among them.

That shift means your primary reference point can no longer be external signs alone. The covenant is now an internal reality.

This relocation created a problem that religion was not prepared for: How do you relate to realities you cannot feel?

When Christ took up residence in you, something irreversible happened in your spirit. But because that change was not sensory, many believers default back to emotional verification: *"I know the Bible says Christ lives in me, but I don't feel Him."* Scripture never promised you would. Instead, it promised that you would know.

You can have indwelling without feeling it. You are required to believe God's witness over your inner noise.

Knowing is not emotional awareness; it is revelatory certainty. It is truth settled at the level of conviction, not sensation.

This is why Paul prays repeatedly, not that believers would feel something, but that the eyes of their understanding would be enlightened. Sight, not sensation, is the issue.

If your inner eyes are not trained, you will keep searching for proof through feelings.

Identity cannot Be Discovered Through Emotion.

If identity is built on feelings, it will always be reactive. If identity is built on revelation, it becomes stable.

The enemy understands this well. He does not need to convince believers that Scripture is false. He only needs to convince them that their feelings are more trustworthy than God's Word.

This was the strategy in the garden: *"Did God really say...?"* And it remains the strategy today: *"Yes, but do you really feel that's true?"*

The moment you answer feelings instead of the Word, you shift from faith to self-interpretation.

Once feelings become the lens through which truth is filtered, identity erodes. Believers begin living as spiritual orphans, saved, but unsure; forgiven, but insecure; accepted, but hesitant.

You can still profess the right doctrine, but you'll feel like you don't belong. This book begins here because nothing else will hold if this is not settled.

You cannot build identity on emotion. You cannot grow spiritually through sensation. You cannot walk in authority if you require emotional confirmation first.

The Kingdom of God is entered by faith, and faith begins where feelings end. Faith does not wait for emotional permission. It responds to divine declaration.

Necessary Reorientation

This chapter does not ask you to deny your feelings. It asks you to demote them. They are valuable servants but terrible masters.

The Christian life begins to stabilize when the Word of God becomes the final reference point, not how you feel today, not how you failed yesterday, not how confident you feel in this moment.

Reality does not change because you feel unsure. Truth does not weaken because you feel distant. Identity does not dissolve because emotions fluctuate.

You do not feel your way into reality. You believe your way into alignment with it. And when belief is settled, feelings eventually follow.

This is how stability is built: you return to what is true before you return to what feels true.

Self-Reflective Questions

1. Where have you been using feelings as proof of whether God is near?
2. What spiritual truth do you say you believe but struggle to live as if it is true?
3. When you feel condemned, what do you usually do next—withdraw, strive, or return to truth?
4. What emotion most often controls your spiritual confidence: fear, shame, discouragement, or anxiety?
5. What would change in your daily walk if God's Word became your final reference point instead of your emotional state?

Chapter 2: The Word As The Only Accurate Mirror

Identity Is Revealed, Not Self-Discovered

Every person eventually builds an identity around a mirror. The only question is: which one? Some individuals gaze into the mirror of their own experiences. Some stare into the mirror of failure. Others look into the mirror of success. Many are drawn to the mirror of culture, family expectations, or religious tradition.

And whatever mirror you choose will begin to shape your self-talk. It will decide what you call "true" about you. It will become the silent judge behind your confidence or your shame.

But Scripture identifies only one mirror that tells the truth about who you are in Christ, and it is not internal. It is revealed.

This is why identity cannot be built on instinct. Instinct is shaped by history. Revelation is shaped by God.

The book of James describes the Word of God as a mirror, not because it inspires self-reflection, but because it reveals objective reality. A mirror does not ask permission. It does not adjust itself to preference. It reflects what is, not what feels true.

A mirror may expose something you would rather ignore, but it does so to restore alignment, not to produce shame.

This is foundational. Identity cannot be discovered by introspection. It must be revealed.

If you only search inward, you will only find what you already believe. But if you look into the Word, you encounter what God has declared.

Why the Human Conscience Is an Unreliable Mirror

Many believers assume their conscience is the primary guide to identity. While conscience is important, it is not authoritative. Scripture tells us plainly that conscience can be weak, defiled, seared, or misinformed.

A conscience can be sincere and still be inaccurate. It can be loud and still be wrong. It can accuse you of what God has already cleansed.

A guilty conscience does not always mean guilt before God. A peaceful conscience does not always mean righteousness before God. Conscience reacts to what it has been trained to believe. If it has been trained under the law, it will accuse even when Christ has acquitted. If it has been trained under fear, it will condemn even when grace has spoken.

This is why some people feel condemned even after repentance, while others feel fine even while drifting. Conscience is not a perfect compass; it is a trained response system.

This is why so many believers remain trapped in cycles of self-assessment:

- "How am I doing spiritually?"
- "Do I feel close to God?"
- "Did I perform well enough today?"

Those questions reveal the mirror being used.

They are not wrong because you care. They are wrong because they assume the answer is found in you.

The Word of God does not ask how you feel about your standing. It declares your standing.

Feelings may indicate your condition. The Word declares your position. Those are not the same thing.

The Bible Is Not a Book of Ideals, It Is a Book of Inheritance

One of the most subtle errors in Christian reading is approaching Scripture as a book of aspiration rather than revelation. Many read the Bible and think:

- "I could never live like that."
- "That must be for especially holy people."
- "That sounds nice, but unrealistic."

That posture belongs to the Old Covenant. Under the New Covenant, Scripture is no longer describing what humans should become; it is describing what has already been accomplished in Christ and imparted to those who are in Him.

If you read the New Testament like a distant goal, you will live in constant frustration. But if you read it like a covenant document, you begin to realize it is describing what is now yours through union.

The Bible is not primarily a moral instruction manual. It is a legal document of inheritance.

It tells you:

- what Christ purchased,
- what has been transferred,
- what is now accessible,
- and what you are authorized to walk in.

It is not simply telling you what to do. It is telling you what has been done and what the finished work means for you.

When believers read Scripture without understanding union, they unconsciously read it as outsiders looking in. They admire faith instead of exercising it. They applaud righteousness instead of receiving it.

They read promises as if they are for "better Christians," instead of realizing the promises were written to people already placed in Christ.

But once you understand that Christ lives in you, the posture changes. Scripture no longer reads as an impossible standard. It reads as a description of available life.

Why Identity Must Precede Application

A mirror is not meant to be admired. It is meant to be acted upon. When you look into a mirror and see dirt on your face, you do not argue with it. You do not attempt to feel cleaner. You respond to what you see.

In the same way, the Word reveals what is true so that life can be aligned accordingly.

The mirror is not condemning you. It is informing you. It is giving you a reference point strong enough to build consistency.

This is why Scripture insists that we be doers of the Word, not hearers only. Hearing without alignment produces self-deception, not because the Word is unclear, but because agreement has not yet become obedience.

One can mentally agree with new ideas while still adhering to an old identity. That is why hearing alone can feel inspiring but leave you unchanged.

But obedience here is not striving. It is alignment.

You do not act to become righteous. You act because righteousness has already been imparted. You do not forgive in order to earn favor.

You forgive because you have been forgiven. You do not resist sin to prove holiness. You resist because sin contradicts your nature.

Identity always comes first. When identity is settled, obedience becomes consistent. When identity is uncertain, obedience becomes exhausting.

The Danger of Reading Scripture From the Wrong Location

Perhaps the greatest mistake believers make is reading the Bible as if Christ were still outside of them.

They read commands as if they were written to powerless humans trying to reach God, rather than to sons already indwelt by Him. They read promises as distant possibilities rather than present possessions.

This produces exhaustion.

The New Testament was written to people who were already in Christ. When that is forgotten, Scripture becomes burdensome instead of liberating.

You will treat inheritance like a goal, and you will treat grace like a wage.

The Word was never meant to crush you. It was meant to reveal you.

It reveals who Christ is, and it reveals who you are because you are in Him.

Why the Mirror Must Be Trusted Over Experience

Experience is powerful, but it is interpretive, not definitive.

Two believers can have identical experiences and draw opposite conclusions. One interprets hardship as abandonment. The other interprets it as refinement. The difference is not the experience; it is the lens.

The Word of God is the only lens that never lies.

When experience contradicts it, it reveals the truth. It speaks with certainty when emotions hesitate. It anchors identity when circumstances fluctuate.

This is why Scripture must be trusted first, not last. It should not serve as a secondary confirmation, but as the primary authority.

When you place experience above the Word, you will keep rewriting your identity. When you place the Word above experience, you begin to interpret life correctly.

When the Word becomes the mirror you trust, something stabilizing happens:

- You stop renegotiating identity daily.
- You stop measuring yourself by performance.
- You stop letting circumstances redefine you.
- You begin to live from revelation rather than reaction.

A Necessary Commitment

This chapter demands a decision, not emotional, but foundational. Will you allow the Word of God to define who you are, even when feelings, memories, and experiences argue otherwise?

Because the argument will come, old memories will speak. Old patterns will try to interpret your life. And in those moments, the mirror you trust will determine whether you stand firm or collapse inward.

If the mirror is compromised, identity will always be fragile. But if the mirror is trusted, identity becomes settled, and settled identity produces authority, peace, and consistency.

And this is where the battle becomes simple: you stop asking, "How do I feel?" and you start asking, "What has God said?"

Self-Reflective Questions

1. Which "mirror" do you use most often to define yourself, experience, failure, success, culture, or the Word?
2. When your conscience accuses you, do you automatically believe it, or do you check it against what God says?
3. Do you read Scripture like a distant ideal or like an inheritance that belongs to you in Christ?
4. What is one command or promise you've been treating as "for others," not for you, and why?
5. What practical change would happen this week if you let the Word define your identity before your emotions speak?

Chapter 3: Hearers, Doers, And The Crisis Of Agreement

When Revelation Becomes Your Normal, Not Just Your Language

One of the most dangerous places a believer can live is between revelation and agreement.

It is a quiet place where you can recognize truth, repeat truth, even defend the truth, and still live as though nothing has changed. This space is not openly rebellious. It is simply unfinished.

This space is subtle. It feels safe. It even feels spiritual. But it produces very little fruit.

James identifies this danger with unsettling clarity when he discusses two types of individuals who examine God's Word: hearers and doers. His concern is not ignorance. It is something far more deceptive: exposure without alignment.

James is not warning us about a lack of information. He is warning about a life that hears revelation but refuses reordering. NKJV anchor: *"But be doers of the word, and not hearers only, deceiving yourselves"* (James 1:22, NKJV). The issue is not hearing. The issue is self-deception—thinking that hearing equals agreement.

A hearer is not someone who rejects truth. A hearer is someone who recognizes truth without rearranging life around it.

A hearer can be moved by truth and remain governed by old patterns. This is why James calls the hearer self-deceived. The hearer is not deceived by false doctrine, but rather by partial obedience.

The deception is not, *"I believe a lie."* The deception is, *"I believed the truth because I liked it, understood it, or felt encouraged by it."*

If the Word consistently comforts you but rarely corrects you, you may be hearing without aligning. If it informs your vocabulary but not your decisions, agreement is incomplete.

Why Agreement Is More than Mental Assent

Many believers assume that agreement with God happens the moment they intellectually affirm Scripture. But biblical agreement is not cognitive assent; it is existential alignment.

Agreement is when God's verdict becomes your inner reference point, not just your outer confession. It is when truth begins to govern what you expect, how you interpret yourself, and what you refuse to tolerate.

Agreement means God's verdict becomes your operating reality. This is why Scripture uses language like *"reckon," "consider,"* and *"count."* These are accounting terms. They describe a deliberate decision to treat something as true, regardless of whether it feels true yet.

Accounting language is intentional. It means you place God's verdict in the "true" category and stop treating your old identity as the default.

To agree with God is to say: *"If God says this is true about me, then I will live as though it is already so."* Not pretending. Not forcing emotion. Not ignoring growth processes. However, it does mean refusing to live as though the old story still governs.

The agreement does not deny the process. It simply refuses to give authority to what has been replaced. It allows growth to happen from the right starting point.

A practical example: if you say you are accepted, but you still approach God cautiously as though you are merely tolerated, your mouth may be agreeing while your posture is resisting. Agreement shows up first in approach, how you come, how you ask, and how you respond when you fail.

The Subtle Self-Deception of Religious Hearing

Religious hearing is dangerous because it feels like growth. People attend teachings on identity, union, righteousness, and inheritance. They enjoy the clarity. They feel encouraged. They even feel hope. But nothing fundamentally shifts, because agreement never crosses the line into alignment.

Inspiration can feel like transformation, but it is not the same thing. Inspiration lifts the moment. Alignment reorders life.

They leave saying:

- "That was powerful."
- "That really helped me."
- "That explains so much."

Yet they continue to:

- pray from insecurity,
- resist sin through willpower,
- approach God cautiously,
- interpret failure as identity,
- and relate to God as though distance still exists.

This is what an unresolved agreement looks like. You know the truth, but you still live by the reflexes of the old narrative.

The tragedy is not a lack of knowledge. It is an unresolved agreement.

James says the hearer looks into the mirror, sees the truth, and then walks away, only to forget what kind of person he is. Forgetting here does not mean mental amnesia. It means functional disregard.

You did not forget the content. You forgot the location you now live in. You returned to the old reference point.

The truth was seen, but it was not allowed to redefine normal life.

If you consistently "receive" the Word but your baseline reactions remain fear, shame, and self-protection, then the Word is still being treated as information instead of identity.

Why Doing Is Not About Effort

When Scripture speaks of being a *"doer of the Word,"* it is not calling believers to religious exertion. It is calling them to align themselves with reality.

Doing is not a spiritual strain. It is spiritual consistency. It means acting in accordance with what God has already declared to be true.

Doing does not involve striving to become something. It means behaving consistently with what already exists. A person who believes they are forgiven is more likely to forgive others. A person who believes they are accepted approaches confidently. A person who believes Christ lives in them yields rather than strains.

That is not perfection. That is alignment.

This is why identity must always precede obedience. Otherwise, obedience becomes compensation, an attempt to earn what God has already given.

The doer is not the one who works harder. The doer is the one who adjusts life to revelation.

When truth confronts a pattern, do you defend the pattern or adjust to the truth? Adjustment is being done. Defense is hearing.

You wake up feeling condemned. A hearer searches for a spiritual "high" to feel clean again. A doer returns to what God has said, thanks Him for cleansing, and moves through the day from acceptance instead of trying to earn it.

The Cost of Agreement

True agreement with God is disruptive. It dismantles coping mechanisms built around guilt. It exposes habits sustained by fear. It confronts religious structures that thrive on performance.

Agreement is not only comforting. It is confrontational. It makes certain behaviors impossible to continue justifying.

This is why many believers unconsciously resist agreement—not because they reject truth, but because truth necessitates reordering.

If you agree that you are righteous, you can no longer:

- relate to God as condemned,
- tolerate cycles of shame,
- justify constant spiritual insecurity.

If you agree that Christ lives in you, you can no longer:

- excuse passivity,
- live as a victim of circumstance,
- wait for permission to walk in authority.

Agreement demands responsibility, not to earn identity, but to live consistently with it. Responsibility in the New Covenant is not pressure. It is stewardship. God is not asking you to produce identity; He is asking you to live from it.

Faith Begins Where Excuses End

Faith is often misunderstood as emotional confidence. In reality, faith is a decisive alignment.

Faith says: *"This is true; therefore, I will act accordingly, even if my emotions lag behind."*

Faith is not ignoring emotion. Faith is refusing emotion the right to veto God's Word.

This is why Scripture says faith without corresponding action is dead. This is not because action generates faith, but because action exposes the existence of faith.

Action does not earn truth. It reveals whether truth has been welcomed into your decisions.

If truth never alters behavior, it has yet to be believed, no matter how often it is affirmed.

Do you use truth to feel encouraged, or do you use truth to reorient your life? Encouragement is good, but reorientation is the goal.

Why This Chapter Is a Turning Point

Up to this point, you have been invited to see identity differently. From this point forward, the question changes, not: *"Is this true?"* but: *"Will I live as though it is?"*

Everything that follows in this book assumes that decision has been made. Without it, identity remains theoretical, and transformation remains delayed. But when agreement is settled, change accelerates, not through striving, but through alignment.

Alignment does not make you new. It enables what is already true to finally govern your actions.

A Line That Must Be Crossed

You cannot indefinitely admire truth without consequence. Eventually, truth demands agreement, or it exposes resistance. This chapter draws a line:

- You are no longer being asked to listen.
- You are being asked to align.

Once alignment begins, identity ceases to be something you learn and becomes something you live from. And when you begin living from truth, growth stops being a struggle for change and becomes the natural outworking of what God has already established.

Self-Reflective Questions

1. Where have you been hearing truth without rearranging your life around it?
2. What truth do you agree with mentally but still struggle to live out daily?
3. Which pattern in your life shows you are still functioning from an old identity story?
4. What is one area where you need to align—not strive—so your actions match what God says is true?
5. What excuse has been protecting you from full agreement, and what would change if you let it go?

Chapter 4: What Actually Happened When You Were Born Again?

Salvation Was Not a Second Chance; It Was a New Creation

Most believers can recount the exact moment of their rebirth. Most people cannot accurately explain what actually happened.

That gap matters because what you believe happened will determine how you live afterward. If you think salvation was mainly a fresh start, you will spend your life trying to improve the old you. If you understand salvation as death and new birth, you will begin living from a different foundation.

Ask the average Christian what salvation accomplished, and the answer is almost always the same: "My sins were forgiven." That statement is not wrong, but it is profoundly incomplete. Forgiveness is precious, but it is not the deepest layer of what occurred. It was possible because something more radical took place.

Forgiveness is not the event of salvation. It is the outcome of something far more radical.

If salvation were merely forgiveness, Christianity would be little more than divine leniency, a holy God agreeing to tolerate flawed people. Sin would remain central, guilt would remain functional, and the believer's primary task would be to manage failure rather than pursue transformation and a deeper relationship with God through faith and grace.

That version of Christianity still keeps the old identity intact. It simply attempts to maintain control over the old identity.

But Scripture presents a much more decisive reality. Salvation did not improve you. It ended you. And what cannot be managed, repaired, or trained must be replaced.

The Gospel Is Not About Correction, It Is About Termination

The New Testament does not describe salvation as moral renovation. It describes it as death.

Paul does not say, *"Your old self was forgiven."* He says, *"Your old self was crucified."* Crucifixion is not repairable. It is execution.

A crucified man is not a man in recovery. A crucified man is finished. That is the point.

This is where religious thinking collapses. Religion prefers modification. God chose eradication.

Religion tries to make the old nature behave better. The gospel declares that the old nature has been put to death.

The old self, the person defined by Adam, sin, independence, and separation, was not rehabilitated. It was put to death.

This is why Scripture insists so forcefully: *"You have died"* (Colossians 3:3, NKJV). That statement is not motivational language. It is a covenant verdict about what happened to the old you.

This is why Scripture continues to emphasize:

"You have died."

"We were buried with Him."

"It is no longer I who live."

These are not metaphors for commitment. They are descriptions of what occurred. They describe a spiritual reality that is true even when your emotions still feel familiar, and your habits still need renewal.

Until this is understood, believers will endlessly try to fix what God has already destroyed.

And that produces a strange kind of frustration: you keep improving what God already ended, and you keep apologizing for what God already replaced.

Why Forgiveness Alone Is Not Enough

Forgiveness deals with guilt. It does not deal with nature.

If salvation stopped at forgiveness, the believer would remain fundamentally unchanged, still a sinner, merely pardoned. Sin would remain normal. Failure would remain expected. Growth would depend almost entirely on discipline and restraint.

That approach creates constant tension, because you are trying to behave like a new person while still believing you are the old person.

But Scripture says something far more disruptive: *"If anyone is in Christ, he is a new creation"* (2 Corinthians 5:17, NKJV). Not a forgiven creation. Not a repaired creation. A new one.

This means the problem God addressed was not merely what you did, but who you were. God did not forgive the old nature. He replaced it.

Grace did not polish Adam. Grace terminated Adamic identity and introduced a new humanity in Christ.

Death Is the Only Door to New Creation

New life requires death. There is no shortcut. This is why Jesus consistently spoke of losing life to find it, not metaphorically, but ontologically. Something had to end before something new could begin.

The gospel is not self-help. It is not self-improvement. It is self-ending and God-beginning.

When Christ died, you were not an observer. You were included. This inclusion is the heart of substitutionary atonement, not merely that Jesus died for you, but that you died with Him.

This is why salvation is not only a gift you receive, but also a location you enter. You were transferred into the reality of what He accomplished.

When he was buried, the old you was buried. When he rose, someone entirely new emerged.

This is not poetry. This is the mechanics of salvation.

And if the mechanics are real, then your old identity is not your default. It is your past.

Why Behavior Management Fails

If salvation is understood only as forgiveness, sin management becomes central. Christians spend their lives resisting what feels natural, constantly suppressing impulses that still seem to define them.

That kind of Christianity is exhausting because it assumes the old nature remains the primary engine, and holiness is only a stronger brake.

But Paul never addresses sin by urging restraint. He addresses it by declaring death: *"How can we who died to sin still live in it?"* That question assumes impossibility, not obligation.

Sin is no longer natural to the believer. It is contradictory.

That does not mean temptation disappears. It means temptation no longer has the right to define you.

When a believer sins, Scripture does not say, *"This is who you are."* It says, *"You were deceived."* Deception is required to act against your nature.

You have to believe something false about yourself to live beneath what is true.

The End of the "Sinner Saved by Grace" Identity

One of the most damaging phrases in modern Christianity is the idea that believers are *"sinners saved by grace."*

It sounds humble. It sounds spiritual. But it contradicts Scripture. You were a sinner. You were saved by grace. But you are no longer a sinner. Scripture consistently calls believers:

- Saints
- Righteous
- Holy
- children of God

Identity language matters. You will live according to what you believe yourself to be.

This is not about arrogance. This is about accuracy. Humility is agreeing with God, not refusing what He has said.

If you see yourself primarily as a sinner, you will sin by faith, because identity governs behavior. But if you see yourself as someone who has died and been raised new, sin becomes an anomaly rather than an expectation.

You stop planning for failure as if it is inevitable, and you start living from the reality that a new nature has been imparted.

Why This Truth Feels So Disruptive

This chapter unsettles religious systems because it removes control mechanisms built on guilt and fear. It shifts the focus from managing behavior to remembering identity.

Religion asks, *"How do I stop sinning?"* The gospel asks, *"Do you know who you are now?"*

That question changes everything.

Because if identity is settled, obedience becomes a response instead of pressure. But if identity is unsettled, obedience becomes performance, and fear becomes motivation.

Necessary Reframing

Salvation is not God giving you another chance. It is God giving you another life.

The old life is not improved. It is gone.

And until that is settled, Christian living will always feel like striving against yourself.

But once it is settled, obedience becomes response, not effort.

And this is where freedom begins: when you stop trying to improve the old you and start agreeing with what God has already done in Christ.

Self-Reflective Questions

1. In what area of your life are you still trying to "improve" the old you instead of living from the new creation?
2. Do you relate to salvation mainly as forgiveness, or do you also see it as death and new birth?
3. When you sin or fail, do you interpret it as identity or as deception against your true nature?
4. What phrases or labels have you been using to describe yourself that may contradict what Scripture calls you?
5. What would change in your daily walk if you truly believed the old life was gone and a new life had begun?

Chapter 5: You Were Not Patched Up, You Were Replaced

The Gospel Ends the Old Life and Introduces a New Source

One of the quiet assumptions beneath much Christian teaching is that salvation is essentially repair work.

That assumption sounds comforting because it allows you to keep the old self and simply hope it can be improved. But the New Testament presents something far more decisive than improvement.

The picture is rarely stated outright, but it is deeply ingrained: humanity was damaged by sin, and God stepped in to fix what was broken. He cleaned us up, improved us, strengthened our weaknesses, and gave us tools to do better next time.

That picture feels hopeful. It also happens to be wrong.

It is wrong because it assumes the old nature is still the main material God is working with. Scripture does not treat the old nature as salvageable. It treats it as finished.

Scripture does not describe salvation as restoration of the old self. It describes it as a replacement. God did not refurbish fallen humanity. He ended it.

This is why salvation is not presented as spiritual self-help. It is presented as death, burial, and resurrection, real events with real consequences for your identity.

Why Repair Was Never an Option

If the old nature could be repaired, the cross would have been unnecessary. The problem was not that humanity needed guidance. Humanity did not need discipline. Humanity did not need education. The problem was nature.

Adam did not merely commit sin; he transmitted a condition. Separation from God became internal, not situational. No amount of moral correction could resolve that.

You can train behavior, but you cannot change nature. Nature produces fruit according to what it is, not according to what it says.

This is why God did not send Jesus primarily as a teacher. He sent Him as a second Adam, a new head, a new source, a new origin.

A teacher can instruct you. A new head can relocate you. A teacher can inform the mind. A new head can transform your life.

When Scripture says Christ came *"in the likeness of sinful flesh,"* it is not suggesting improvement. It is announcing termination followed by replacement. The old humanity could not be healed. It had to be put to death.

That is why the gospel is not presented as God helping Adam behave. It is presented as God introducing a new humanity in Christ.

Why the Cross Was Not About Making You Better

If the goal of salvation were self-improvement, the gospel would be about motivation. Instead, it is about identification. You were not invited to admire the cross. You were included in it.

The cross is not merely an event you honor. It is an event you were part of. This is why Paul speaks with certainty, not suggestion.

Paul's language is absolute: *"I have been crucified with Christ… it is no longer I who live, but Christ lives in me"* (Galatians 2:20, NKJV).

These statements make no sense in a repair model. They only make sense in a replacement model. The "I" Paul refers to, the Adamic self defined by separation, performance, and self-rule, no longer exists.

Salvation is not God helping the old you succeed. It is God ending the old you entirely.

If the old "I" remains the center of your Christian life, you will interpret the gospel as assistance instead of replacement, and you will live as though you are still the source.

Why the "Improved Self" Model Fails in Practice

When believers see salvation as improvement, several things inevitably happen:

1. Sin remains central. The Christian life becomes primarily about sin avoidance rather than Christ's expression.
2. Guilt remains functional. Failure feels personal, not circumstantial. Shame becomes instructional.
3. Growth feels exhausting. Progress depends on effort, discipline, and emotional stamina.
4. Identity remains fragile. Confidence rises and falls based on performance.

Even when outward behavior improves, the inner story often remains the same: *"I am still basically broken, but I'm trying harder."* That story keeps you in self-focus, not Christ-focus.

This is not accidental. You cannot live victoriously while clinging to an identity God has already discarded. Trying to improve the old self is like polishing a gravestone. It may look better, but it is still dead.

A gravestone can be decorated, but it cannot be resurrected. The gospel does not decorate death. It delivers you from it.

The Radical Nature of Replacement

Replacement means something far more invasive than repair. It means:

- a new source of life
- a new spiritual DNA
- a new operating system

Replacement also means your starting point has changed. You are no longer starting from "broken, trying to become whole." You are starting from being made new and learning to walk.

This is why Scripture uses language like *"born again," "new creation," "made alive,"* and *"created in righteousness."* None of these words describes improvement. They describe origination.

"If anyone is in Christ, he is a new creation" (2 Corinthians 5:17, NKJV).

You are not the old person behaving differently. You are a new person learning how to live.

That learning process matters because habits may linger, memories may speak loudly, and emotions may argue, but those things do not define what happened. They only reveal what still needs renewing.

Why This Truth Is Often Resisted

Replacement is threatening because it removes familiar reference points. If the old self is gone, you can no longer:

- define yourself by past trauma
- excuse behavior as "just how I am."
- negotiate identity through performance
- cling to false humility rooted in self-disdain

Replacement demands a new way of seeing yourself, and responsibility to live from it.

It also removes your most common hiding place: the ability to blame your old identity for what you now choose to tolerate. Replacement calls you into ownership, not ownership of shame, but ownership of truth.

This is why some believers unconsciously prefer the improvement model. It allows them to keep their old selves while hoping God will make it manageable.

But the gospel offers something better.

It offers freedom from the old self, not management of it.

From Self-Management to Self-Surrender

Christian maturity is not about managing the old self more effectively. It is about yielding to the new life within.

This is why Paul does not exhort believers to become new. He exhorts them to put off old ways of thinking and live from what is already true.

He is not asking you to manufacture a new identity. He is urging you to stop living from an identity that has already been judged and replaced.

You do not surrender in order to become new. You surrender because you already are.

Surrender is not a payment. It is an agreement. It is stepping into what God has already established.

A Necessary Shift in Language

How you speak about yourself matters. When believers continually refer to themselves as broken, struggling sinners trying to improve, they reinforce an identity God has already removed.

The gospel invites a different language, not arrogance, but accuracy.

You are not patched up. You are not upgraded. You are not rehabilitated. You were replaced.

And the life you now live is not yours alone; it is Christ's life expressed through you.

This does not make you flawless overnight. It makes your foundation different. And when the foundation is right, growth becomes the outworking of truth instead of the chase for worth.

Self-Reflective Questions

1. Where do you still consider salvation to be repair rather than replacement, and how does that show up in your daily life?
2. What part of you still believes the "old self" is the real you, even though Scripture says it ended?
3. When you fail, do you interpret it as proof of identity or evidence that your mind still needs renewal?
4. What phrases do you use to describe yourself that might reinforce an identity God has already removed?
5. What would change this week if you consistently approached God as someone made new, not someone trying to become new?

Chapter 6: Forgiveness Is Not The Gospel, New Creation Is

Forgiveness Opens the Door, but Resurrection Life Is the Point

The belief that forgiveness is the center of the gospel is one of the most misunderstood and limiting ideas.

This misunderstanding is subtle because forgiveness is real, necessary, and deeply emotional. It feels like the climax because guilt is loud. But the gospel does not stop where guilt stops.

Forgiveness is precious. Forgiveness is necessary. Forgiveness is powerful. But forgiveness is not the gospel.

Forgiveness is the entry point that makes union possible. It removes the obstacles to a relationship, but it does not encompass the entirety of salvation.

When forgiveness is treated as the destination rather than the doorway, the Christian life stalls at the level of guilt management instead of advancing into transformation. The gospel does not culminate in pardon. It culminates in a new creation.

Until that is settled, you will keep returning to forgiveness as if it must be re-earned instead of living from what has already been made new.

Why Forgiveness Alone Leaves Identity Intact

Forgiveness deals with actions. New creation deals with being.

A forgiven criminal is still the same person, only released from penalty. If salvation stopped at forgiveness, the believer would remain fundamentally unchanged, merely spared consequences.

That model makes salvation feel like release from punishment rather than transfer into a new life. It produces relief, but not transformation.

That model quietly preserves the old identity:

- still Adamic
- still self-centered
- still sin-conscious
- still performance-oriented

It produces Christians who are grateful, but not free.

They live forgiven, yet hesitant. Accepted, yet insecure. Loved, yet unsure. This is because forgiveness alone does not address nature.

And if nature is not addressed, sin remains the "normal" pull, and holiness feels like constant resistance instead of inward alignment.

The Gospel Does Not Ignore Sin, It Outgrows It

Religion often assumes that emphasizing new creation minimizes the seriousness of sin. Scripture does the opposite. The gospel does not trivialize sin; it defeats it at the root.

Sin is not primarily a behavior problem. It is a natural problem.

God did not merely forgive sin; He removed the sinner. This is why the gospel does not mean that God simply overlooks wrongdoing. It means God ended the old humanity and introduced a new one in Christ.

This is why the cross is central. Sin was not excused; it was judged. But the judgment did not fall on actions alone; it fell on the old humanity itself.

"Our old man was crucified with Him" (Romans 6:6, NKJV).

Forgiveness without death would leave sin powerful. Death stripped sin of jurisdiction.

Jurisdiction is the key issue. Sin rules where it has authority. Death ends authority. Resurrection introduces a new authority and a new life.

Why Paul Preaches Identity, Not Behavior

When addressing moral failure, Paul rarely begins with instruction. He begins with identity:

"Do you not know…?"

"Remember who you are…"

"You have died…"

"You were raised…"

He does not say, "Try harder." He says, "You are someone else now."

Paul understood something religion often forgets: people do not rise above the level of their identity.

If believers see themselves primarily as forgiven sinners, sin remains normal. If they see themselves as new creations, sin becomes foreign. This is not denial. It is recalibration.

Recalibration means your inner reference point changes. You stop treating sin as your natural language and start treating it as a contradiction that requires deception to continue.

The Power of New Creation Language

Language shapes imagination. Imagination shapes expectation. Expectation shapes behavior.

So the way you describe yourself today is not neutral. It becomes a blueprint for what you tolerate tomorrow.

This is why Scripture relentlessly uses new-creation language:

born of God, partakers of the divine nature, and created in righteousness and true holiness.

These phrases are not inspirational metaphors. They are ontological statements—descriptions of what you now are.

Their purpose is to establish identity, not to embellish sermons.

When believers continue to describe themselves internally as broken sinners, they unknowingly resist the very transformation they pray for.

Humility is not self-degradation. Humility is agreement with God. And God says something astonishing about you.

Humility does not mean you deny what Christ accomplished. It means you stop arguing with God's verdict and begin living from it.

Why Forgiveness Is a Door, Not a Destination

Forgiveness removes guilt so that union can occur.

It clears the ground for something far greater: Christ dwelling in you. The gospel does not merely clean the house. It makes the house habitable for God.

If forgiveness were the goal, the Christian life would be about staying clean. But Scripture points to something far more intimate: participation.

You were not allowed to stand at a distance. You were forgiven to become a dwelling place.

This is why the New Covenant promise was never merely forgiveness. It was indwelling:

"I will put My Spirit within you" (Ezekiel 36:27, NKJV).

Forgiveness opens the door. New creation walks through it.

And once the door is opened, you are not meant to remain on the threshold. You are meant to live from the new reality within.

The Tragedy of Forgiveness-Centered Christianity

When forgiveness becomes the center:

Prayer becomes apology-heavy.

Worship becomes remorse-driven.

Growth becomes slow and fragile.

Authority becomes rare.

Believers live circling the cross, never stepping into the resurrection.

While God is calling them into new life, new identity, and new authority, they keep returning to cleansing as if cleansing is the entire story.

But the gospel does not end at the cross. It moves through it.

Death was necessary. Burial was final. Resurrection was the goal.

If the cross deals with what ended, the resurrection reveals what began.

Why Resurrection Language Matters

Resurrection does not restore the old life. It inaugurates a new one.

This is why Scripture insists:

You were made alive.

You were raised with Christ.

Your life is now hidden with Him.

Hidden does not mean inaccessible. It means secure, rooted, and inseparable.

Hidden means your life is no longer anchored in your emotions, your past, or your performance. It is anchored in Christ Himself.

A Reorientation That Changes Everything

You are not primarily someone who sins and gets forgiven. You are someone who lives from a new source.

When this settles, everything shifts:

Sin loses fascination.

Holiness becomes natural.

Obedience becomes responsive.

Authority becomes normal.

Not because you are strong—but because the old you is gone, and Christ lives in you.

This is where freedom becomes practical. You stop fighting to become new and start learning to live from what is already true.

Where This Takes Us Next

If forgiveness is not the center and new creation is, then a crucial question emerges: Where is this new life located?

The answer takes us into the most repeated and most ignored phrase in the New Testament: "in Christ."

That is where we go next.

Self-Reflective Questions

1. In your daily thinking, do you treat forgiveness as the goal or as the doorway into new life?
2. Where do you still relate to yourself primarily as a forgiven sinner instead of a new creation?
3. What does "new creation" need to change in the way you pray, especially after failure?
4. Which phrase best describes your current focus: guilt management or identity alignment, and why?
5. What would shift this week if you truly believed that the point of the gospel is resurrection life, not constant self-correction?

Chapter 7: A New Species, Not An Improved Humanity

New in Kind, New in Source, New in Nature

When Scripture declares that the believer is a new creation, it is making one of the most radical statements in all of theology. Yet because the phrase is familiar, its force is often missed.

Familiar language can become dull language. We hear the phrase so often that we forget it was meant to shock. *"New creation"* is not a poetic compliment. It is a declaration of what God has done to human identity in Christ.

Most believers hear *"new creation"* and assume it means a better version of the old self, more disciplined, more spiritual, more obedient. But that interpretation does not survive careful reading. The language of new creation does not describe enhancement. It describes origination.

Christianity does not announce the improvement of humanity. It announces the emergence of a new kind of humanity.

That means the gospel is not primarily God upgrading your behavior. It is God introducing a different life into you, one that did not come from Adam.

Why "New Creation" Means Something Entirely New

The term translated as *"new"* in *"new creation"* does not mean "new in time," as in recent. It means new in kind, something that did not previously exist.

It is the difference between repainting an old house and building a new one. One is modification. The other is origination.

This is the same word used to describe the new covenant, the new man, and the new heavens and earth. This is not a refurbished version of the old covenant. It is something of an entirely different order.

In other words, God did not take fallen humanity and upgrade it. He introduced a different source of life altogether. And because the source is different, the nature is different. The life you now live does not start with you; it starts with Christ.

This is why Scripture refers to believers as:

- born of God
- born of the Spirit
- born from above

Birth language matters. Birth does not modify; it produces.

Birth also creates a new point of origin. That is why Christianity is not about turning the old you into a better version of yourself. It is about becoming someone who came from above.

Why Improved Humanity Could Never Carry God's Life

The life of God cannot inhabit Adamic nature. This is a critical point. No matter how disciplined, educated, or morally refined humanity becomes, it remains incompatible with divine life. The problem is not behavior; it is origin.

Even the best version of Adam is still Adam. And Adam cannot carry what only Christ can carry.

This is why Jesus told Nicodemus that being religious, sincere, and knowledgeable was not enough. Something more drastic was required: *"You must be born again."* Not trained again. Not refined again. Born again.

Until origin changes, life cannot.

If the root stays the same, the fruit will eventually reveal it.

The Second Adam and the Birth of a New Humanity

Scripture presents Christ not merely as Savior, but as the last Adam. Adam was not just a man; he was a source. Humanity flowed from him and shared his nature. When Adam fell, that nature transmitted separation.

Christ came as a new source. When He rose from the dead, He did not simply return to life. He emerged as the head of a new humanity, one no longer defined by separation, but by union with God.

This is why resurrection is not only proof that Jesus lives. It is the announcement that a new humanity has begun.

This is why Scripture consistently speaks of believers as being *in Christ.* It is the source language. Just as humanity was once *in Adam,* it is now possible to be *in Christ.* And the source determines nature.

You do not merely follow Christ. You are relocated into Him.

Why This Changes the Way We Understand Sin

If believers are merely improved humans, sin remains normal. It is expected, explained, and managed. But if believers are new creations, sin becomes incongruent.

This does not mean believers are without sin. It means sin no longer fits. Sin becomes something you can fall into, but it is no longer something you belong to.

When a fish ends up on land, it struggles, not because it is wicked, but because it is out of place. Likewise, believers sin not because it defines them, but because they act against their nature.

This reframes repentance. Repentance is not groveling for acceptance. It is returning to alignment with who you truly are.

Repentance is not earning your way back into a relationship. It is coming back into agreement with your new identity.

Why Holiness Is Not Heroic

Religion often presents holiness as heroic effort, the result of discipline, sacrifice, and willpower. But in the new creation, holiness is organic.

A tree does not struggle to bear fruit consistent with its nature. It bears fruit because of what it is. In the same way, holiness is not something the believer forces. It emerges when the new life within is allowed to express itself.

This is why Scripture says, *"Walk by the Spirit, and you will not fulfill the desires of the flesh."*

It does not say, "Suppress the flesh harder." It says, "Live from the new source."

The Holy Spirit does not merely help you behave better. He empowers you to live from what you have become.

Why This Threatens Religious Control

A new-species understanding of salvation removes fear-based control. If believers are truly new creations, guilt loses leverage, shame loses authority, and fear loses motivational power.

And when fear no longer drives you, religion can no longer manipulate you.

Religion often prefers the improvement model because it keeps believers dependent on external systems of correction. But new creation shifts the locus of transformation inside.

This is not dangerous freedom. It is a restored design.

God never intended His children to be managed from the outside. He intended them to live from a transformed inside.

External rules can restrain behavior, but only internal life can produce lasting change.

From Self-Improvement to Self-Expression

The Christian life is not about becoming someone else. It is about allowing who you already are in Christ to be expressed.

This is why Paul speaks of putting on the new self, not creating it, but living from what already exists.

You are not chasing identity. You are learning how to walk it out.

And walking it out means your choices begin to match your source. Your habits begin to align with your nature. Your life begins to reflect the life that is within you.

A Line That Cannot Be Blurred

You are either:

1. an improved sinner trying to behave better, or
2. a new creation learning to live from a new source.

Those two models produce radically different lives.

One produces exhaustion. The other produces freedom.

One produces cycles of guilt. The other produces growth.

One keeps the believer focused on self. The other fixes the believer's gaze on Christ within.

And the model you believe will quietly become the life you live.

Where This Leads Next

If a new humanity now exists, and if believers are part of it, then one question becomes unavoidable: Where is this new life located?

The answer introduces us to the most repeated, yet most neglected, phrase in the New Testament: "in Christ."

That is where we go next.

Self-Reflective Questions

1. Do you tend to think of salvation as improvement or as origination into a new kind of life?
2. Why do you still act as if your old source is the real source, even though Scripture says you are new?
3. When you fall into sin, do you interpret it as identity or as acting out of place compared to who you are now?

4. What area of your life would look different if you truly believed holiness is organic to the new nature?
5. Which model has shaped your Christian life more: "an improved sinner" or "a new creation," and what has it produced in you?

Chapter 8: The Geography Of Salvation: What It Means To Be "In Christ"

Location Is Not Symbolic; It Is the Foundation of Identity

Most believers understand salvation in terms of events, the cross, forgiveness, justification, and new birth. Far fewer understand salvation in terms of location. That is why many believers know what happened but still live as if they are standing outside of it, because they have not learned to think in "where" language, only "what" language.

Yet the New Testament speaks relentlessly in geographical language. You are not merely forgiven by Christ. You are not merely taught by Christ. You are not merely helped by Christ. You are in Christ.

This is not a minor wording choice; it is the primary way the New Testament describes your existence, and it is meant to settle your position before it ever addresses your behavior.

This phrase appears dozens of times in the New Testament, not as poetic ornamentation, but as the primary descriptor of Christian existence. It tells us where our life now resides. Identity is not only about who you are. It is also about where you are positioned.

Why Location Determines Identity

In every realm of life, location determines access, authority, and experience. A citizen living outside a country does not enjoy the same privileges as one living within it. The laws may exist, the benefits may be real, but location determines participation. The difference is not whether the privileges exist; it is whether you are positioned where those privileges apply.

In the same way, the New Testament does not merely announce what Christ has accomplished; it announces where believers have been placed as a result. Salvation is not only a legal declaration. It is a relocation of life.

Scripture says:

- "You are in Christ Jesus."
- "Your life is hidden with Christ in God."
- "You have been seated with Him in heavenly places."

These are not metaphors for inspiration. They are descriptions of current spiritual positions. They explain why the Christian life is not primarily about reaching God, but about learning to live from where God has already placed you.

From "With God" to "In Christ"

Under the Old Covenant, God was with His people. That was revolutionary for its time. The presence of God traveled with Israel, hovered over the tabernacle, and later filled the temple. But the distance remained. God was near, but external, present, but not internal.

The best the Old Covenant could offer was proximity. It could bring God near, but it could not bring God within.

The New Covenant collapses that distance entirely. God is no longer merely with you. He has placed you in Christ, and Christ in you. This double union eliminates separation on every level.

It means you are not trying to enter the relationship; you are living from inside it, because the union has already been established.

You are not approaching God from the outside. You are living from within the relationship.

Why "In Christ" Replaces Self-Definition

Once you understand that you are in Christ, self-definition changes. Your identity is no longer anchored in:

- your past
- your failures
- your ethnicity
- your education
- your personality
- your spiritual résumé

It is anchored in location. And location overrides history.

Where you are now matters more than where you came from. This does not erase your story, but it dethrones it. Your history becomes context, not identity.

This is why Scripture does not say, "If anyone is forgiven, he is something better." It says, *"If anyone is in Christ, he is a new creation."*

The defining factor is not improvement; it is placement.

Why Heaven Treats You According to Location

Here is a truth that unsettles religious thinking: Heaven does not interact with you as an isolated individual. It interacts with you as someone who is in Christ.

This means your standing before God is not evaluated independently. It is evaluated through a union.

When Christ is accepted, you are accepted.

When Christ is righteous, you are righteous.

When Christ is seated, you are seated.

This is why your confidence is meant to rest on His position, not your performance, because your access is determined by location, not emotional readiness.

This is not mystical exaggeration. It is covenantal logic. In a covenant, what belongs to one belongs to the other.

God does not see you apart from Christ because you no longer exist apart from Him.

Why This Ends Comparison and Competition

Comparison thrives where identity is self-derived. When believers define themselves by performance, gifting, or maturity, insecurity is inevitable.

There will always be someone who appears more disciplined, more gifted, or more effective. But location-based identity dissolves comparison.

You are not competing for a position. You already have one. You are not striving for acceptance. You are already the accepted one.

And when identity is settled, you can celebrate others without feeling diminished, because your worth is not being measured against their progress.

This produces humility without inferiority and confidence without arrogance.

Why "In Christ" Changes the Way You Read Scripture

Once the location is settled, Scripture reads differently.

Commands stop sounding like external demands and begin sounding like descriptions of what is now possible. Promises stop feeling aspirational and begin feeling accessible.

You stop reading the Bible as someone trying to get closer to God. You read it as someone learning how to live from where you already are.

That shift is not a small adjustment; it is the difference between reading Scripture as a distance-based religion and reading Scripture as covenant reality.

This shift alone resolves countless theological tensions.

The End of Distance-Based Christianity

Much Christian frustration comes from living as though distance still exists. Believers pray as though God is far. They worship as though access is limited. They struggle as though help is external.

But distance was removed at the cross.

You are not on the outside looking in. You are not approaching cautiously. You are not hoping to qualify.

You are in Christ.

And because you are in Christ, you do not ask for access as if it must be granted; you learn to live from access because it already exists.

A Necessary Question

If this is true, and Scripture insists that it is, then a crucial question arises: if remembered daily, how would this location change everything?

- How do you pray?
- How do you face temptation?
- How do you interpret failure?
- How do you approach authority?
- How do you see yourself?

The Christian life does not begin with effort. It begins with location awareness.

Effort without location produces striving. Location without awareness produces inconsistency. But when location is remembered, effort becomes cooperation instead of pressure.

Where This Takes Us Next

If being *"in Christ"* defines our position, then the next truth must be faced honestly:

Why does God treat us the way He treats Jesus?

The answer leads us directly into righteousness, not as behavior, but as legal standing.

Self-Reflective Questions

1. In your daily life, where do you still think and pray as if you are "outside" rather than "in Christ"?
2. What area of your identity do you still define by history or performance instead of by spiritual location?
3. How would your confidence change if you believed heaven interacts with you through union, not independent evaluation?
4. Where has comparison been draining you, and how would location-based identity dissolve that pressure?
5. If you remembered "I am in Christ" before every major decision this week, what would change in how you respond?

Chapter 9: Righteousness: A Legal Verdict, Not An Emotional State

When Heaven Declares You Right, Feelings Stop Negotiating Your Standing

Few words have been more spiritualized, moralized, and misunderstood than the word *"righteousness."* For many believers, righteousness is experienced as a fluctuating internal condition, something felt strongly on good days and doubted on bad ones.

That is why so many people live with a quiet instability: they feel confident when they feel "clean," and they feel distant when they feel "off," even though neither feeling changes what Christ has done.

But Scripture never presents righteousness as a feeling. It presents it as a verdict. Righteousness is not how you feel about yourself. It is how heaven has declared you legally. And a legal declaration does not wait for your emotions to approve it before it becomes effective.

Until this distinction is settled, believers will live in constant internal negotiation, confident one moment, condemned the next, never fully at rest, never fully assured.

Why Righteousness Is a Courtroom Term

Righteousness belongs to the language of law, not emotion. To be righteous means to be declared in right standing before a judge. It does not describe internal sensation; it describes legal status.

That is why the New Testament uses courtroom words like *"justified,"* *"acquitted,"* *"charge,"* *"condemnation,"* and *"verdict."* It is teaching you to think legally about your standing, not emotionally about your worth.

In Scripture, justification is not God pretending you are innocent. It is God declaring that the case against you has been conclusively settled, and not in your favor, but in Christ's.

The evidence was not dismissed; it was answered. The penalty was not ignored; it was absorbed.

This is why Paul asks with confidence, *"Who shall bring a charge against God's elect?"* That question is not poetic. It is juridical. Charges require jurisdiction. Accusations require standing. And Scripture's answer is clear: there is none.

"Who shall bring a charge against God's elect? It is God who justifies" (Romans 8:33, NKJV).

When the Judge has spoken, the courtroom is not waiting for a second opinion.

Why Feelings Cannot Define Righteousness

If righteousness were emotional, it would be unstable. If it were behavioral, it would be fragile. But righteousness is positional.

It exists whether you feel it or not, whether you performed well today or not, and whether you succeeded or failed.

Feelings can report your internal condition, but they cannot reverse your covenant position.

This is why Scripture dares to say, *"There is therefore now no condemnation to those who are in Christ Jesus"* (Romans 8:1, NKJV).

"Now" does not mean "on good days." It means currently, continuously, and without interruption.

Condemnation requires a legal basis. Righteousness removes that basis entirely.

Why Failure Does Not Revoke Righteousness

This is where many believers stumble. They assume that failure cancels righteousness, that sin revokes standing, and that guilt signals lost favor.

But Scripture never supports this logic.

Failure affects fellowship, not status.

Growth, not identity.

Experience, not verdict.

Failure may disrupt your peace, but it does not rewrite God's declaration. It may expose immaturity, but it does not erase sonship.

If righteousness were revoked by failure, salvation would be probation, not covenant.

But righteousness is not maintained by performance. It is imputed by grace.

Imputed means credited to your account because of another, not earned by you, and therefore not fragile in your hands.

This does not excuse sin. It outgrows it.

A child's misbehavior does not change parentage. It changes alignment. In the same way, repentance is not trying to earn your way back into righteousness; it is returning to agreement with the righteousness already given.

Why Condemnation Is the Enemy's Primary Weapon

The enemy does not need to tempt believers if he can first condemn them.

Condemnation erodes confidence.

It weakens prayer.

It silences authority.

It paralyzes action.

This is why Scripture links accusation directly to Satan. He is not called the tempter primarily, but the accuser.

Accusation is strategic because it targets identity. Once you believe you are "not right," you will begin living like someone who does not belong.

Accusation thrives where identity is uncertain. Once a believer accepts condemnation, they begin relating to God from a posture of distance, hoping for mercy rather than standing in confidence.

But righteousness silences accusation permanently.

A condemned person negotiates. A justified person approaches.

Why God Is Not "In a Good Mood" Toward You

Many believers relate to God as though His disposition toward them changes daily, pleased one moment, disappointed the next.

But God's disposition toward you is anchored in Christ, not your behavior.

Because you are in Christ, God's posture toward you is stable. He does not fluctuate between acceptance and rejection. He does not oscillate between favor and displeasure.

He sees you through the righteousness of His Son.

This does not mean God ignores growth, correction, or maturity. It means His love is not hanging on your performance like a fragile thread.

This does not minimize holiness. It establishes it.

Only a secure identity produces sustainable holiness. Fear-driven holiness produces hiddenness. Identity-driven holiness produces consistency.

Righteousness and Confidence in Prayer

Scripture directly connects righteousness to boldness.

"The righteous are bold as a lion."

Boldness does not come from self-confidence. It comes from legal certainty. When you know there is no case against you, you approach without hesitation, not arrogantly, but freely.

Confidence is not you convincing yourself you are worthy; it is you agreeing that Christ is worthy and that you are in Him.

This is why Scripture says, *"We have confidence to enter the Most Holy Place."*

Confidence is not personality-driven. It is verdict-driven.

If you wait to feel confident before you pray, you have made emotion your judge. But if you pray from righteousness, feelings learn to follow truth instead of leading it.

Why This Truth Must Be Protected

Righteousness by grace is often attacked, not because it encourages sin, but because it removes fear as a motivator.

Fear can produce compliance. It cannot produce a transformation.

God does not govern His children through threat. He governs through identity.

When fear is removed, love becomes the motive. And when love becomes the motive, obedience becomes a response instead of a strategy for survival.

A Final Clarification

You are not becoming righteous. You have been made righteous.

You are not trying to maintain standing. Your standing has been secured.

You are not hoping condemnation will lift. It has already been removed.

This is why rest is not laziness; rest is the correct response to a finished verdict.

When this truth settles, striving gives way to rest, and rest becomes the environment where Christ's life flows freely.

Where This Leads Next

If righteousness is settled legally, then the next truth must be faced honestly:

Why does Christ now live in us, and what does that actually mean?

That takes us into the heart of the union.

Self-Reflective Questions

1. Where have you been treating righteousness like a feeling instead of a legal verdict?
2. When you fail, do you tend to withdraw from God, or do you return to what heaven has declared about you?
3. What does "no condemnation" practically need to change in the way you pray and think this week?
4. In what area has accusation been shaping your identity, and what would it look like to silence it with the verdict of righteousness?
5. If you truly believed God's posture toward you is anchored in Christ and not in your daily performance, what would change in your obedience and peace?

Chapter 10: "Christ In You": The End Of Distance

God Did Not Draw Near; He Moved In

If *"in Christ"* tells us where we are, then *"Christ in you"* tells us who is present. Location establishes position, but presence establishes daily reality.

If you only understand *"in Christ"* intellectually, you may still live as if God is far. But once you grasp *"Christ in you,"* distance-based Christianity collapses.

This phrase represents one of the greatest shifts in all of redemptive history, and one of the most under-experienced realities in Christian life.

Many believers affirm it doctrinally, yet continue to live as though God were distant, external, and intermittently involved.

That contradiction is not usually rebellion; it is often habit. People live the way they have learned to live, even after the covenant reality has changed.

But Scripture is unambiguous: *"Christ in you, the hope of glory"* (Colossians 1:27, NKJV).

This is not poetic language. It is relational finality. Distance has been eliminated, not managed, not minimized, but removed entirely.

From Visitation to Habitation

Under the Old Covenant, God visited His people. His presence came upon prophets, rested temporarily on kings, and departed when conditions were violated. A relationship existed, but permanence did not.

Even at its most glorious moments, the Old Covenant still carried a kind of distance. God's presence was real, but it was not the normal daily reality of the average person.

The New Covenant introduces something unprecedented: God does not visit. He dwells.

The Spirit of God does not come and go. He takes up residence. This is why Scripture says believers are not merely followers of Christ, but temples of the Holy Spirit.

Temple language is not symbolic. It is locational. A temple is where a god lives.

Christianity does not proclaim a God who occasionally shows up. It proclaims a God who has moved in.

And once He moves in, your life is no longer defined by trying to reach Him, but by learning to respond to Him.

Why Indwelling Changes Everything

If Christ lives in you, then Christian living cannot be external. It cannot be:

- rule-driven
- motivation-dependent
- willpower-based
- personality-centered

Those approaches assume distance. Indwelling redefines the entire paradigm.

External systems can guide behavior for a time, but they cannot produce the life of Christ. Only indwelling can do that, because only indwelling changes the source.

You are not trying to live like Christ. You are learning how to yield to Christ, living His life through you.

This is why Paul does not say, "I try to imitate Christ better." He says, "Christ lives in me."

Imitation belongs to distance. Expression belongs to a union.

Imitation copies from outside. Expression flows from within.

That difference changes everything about how you approach growth.

Why Many Believers Live as Though Christ Is Absent

The tragedy is not that Christ is absent. It is that believers are unaware.

Awareness is the issue, not presence. Presence is a covenant reality; awareness is a practiced response.

Christ does not become more present when you pray. You become more aware.

He does not enter when you worship. You recognize Him.

He does not arrive when circumstances improve. You yield.

This misunderstanding leads believers to spend their lives trying to "get God to show up," when Scripture declares He already has.

The Christian life is not about summoning God. It is about surrendering to the One who is already there.

And surrender is not weakness. Surrender is an agreement with reality.

Why Power Is Not External

Many believers pray for power as though it were something to be delivered from heaven. But Scripture says:

"His divine power has given to us all things that pertain to life and godliness" (2 Peter 1:3, NKJV).

Power is not a future download. It is a present indwelling reality.

This does not mean believers automatically walk in power. It means power must be recognized, trusted, and yielded to.

A person may live in a house fully wired for electricity and still sit in darkness if they never flip the switch. The power exists, but it is not expressed.

The issue is not supply. It is awareness and alignment.

And alignment begins when you stop asking God to send what He has already placed within you.

Why Dependence Replaces Self-Effort

Indwelling shifts the definition of strength.

Strength is no longer the ability to push harder. It is the willingness to depend fully.

This is why Paul celebrates weakness, not as failure, but as clarity. Weakness exposes the limits of self-effort and creates space for Christ's life to be expressed.

Weakness becomes dangerous only when it turns into self-pity. But when weakness becomes dependence, it becomes a doorway for Christ's strength to be revealed.

Self-effort competes with indwelling. Dependence cooperates with it.

Christian maturity is not about becoming more capable. It is becoming more yielding.

You do not mature by becoming more self-sufficient. You mature by becoming more Christ-dependent.

Why This Ends Performance-Based Faith

Performance assumes that God evaluates you based on output. Indwelling declares that God expresses Himself through relationship.

You do not earn His presence. You host it.

And hosting does not mean you control Him. It means you make room for Him.

It means you stop crowding the space with anxious striving and allow His life to lead.

This does not lead to passivity. It leads to participation.

Christ does not live in you, so you can do nothing. He lives in you so that He can do what you could never do alone.

Participation means you act, but you act from the union. You move, but you move with dependence. You obey, but obedience becomes a response instead of pressure.

The End of Spiritual Loneliness

One of the most painful realities among believers is spiritual loneliness, the feeling of walking alone, making decisions without divine nearness, and struggling without support.

But indwelling eliminates loneliness at the root.

You are never abandoned.

Never unsupported.

Never disconnected.

Even when emotions are silent, presence remains.

This does not mean you will always feel close to God. It means you are never actually far.

Loneliness is often the emotion of distance, but indwelling changes the truth beneath that emotion. Presence remains even when the feeling does not.

A Necessary Reorientation of Expectation

If Christ lives in you, then the Christian life is not about chasing experiences. It is about cultivating awareness.

You do not ask, "Where is God?" You ask, "How do I yield here?"

You do not say, "God, come help me." You say, "Christ, live through me."

This subtle shift transforms prayer, obedience, and daily life.

It also changes how you interpret silence. Silence no longer means absence. It means you must return to truth and yield where you are.

Where This Takes Us Next

If Christ lives in us, then the Christian life cannot be lived through striving. It must be lived through inheritance and authority.

The question now becomes: if Christ is present within us, what does that mean for access, provision, and authority?

That is where we go next.

Self-Reflective Questions

1. Where in your daily life do you still live as if God is distant instead of indwelling?
2. When you pray, do you tend to ask God to "come," or do you practice yielding to the One already present?
3. What area of your life shows the strongest dependence on willpower rather than dependence on Christ within you?
4. How would your choices change if you believed power is present within you and not delayed in the future?
5. What practical step can you take this week to cultivate awareness of "Christ in you" during ordinary moments?

Chapter 11: Inheritance: Access, Not Achievement

You Do Not Earn What Belongs Already Granted

One of the most persistent distortions in Christian thinking is the belief that spiritual life operates on achievement rather than inheritance.

That distortion is subtle because achievement is how most of life works: you study to pass, you work to get paid, and you perform to be recognized. If you carry that mindset into salvation, you will treat God like an employer instead of a Father, and treat prayer like a transaction instead of a relationship.

Believers often relate to God as workers trying to earn wages instead of sons learning how to access what already belongs to them.

Prayer becomes effort. Faith becomes persuasion. Obedience becomes currency.

And once obedience becomes currency, peace becomes rare, because you are constantly evaluating whether you have "done enough" to qualify.

But Scripture never frames the Christian life around earning. It frames it around inheritance. Inheritance does not reward performance. It recognizes a relationship.

Inheritance answers the question achievement can never settle: *Do you belong?*

Why the Language of Inheritance Matters

The New Testament does not hesitate to use legal and familial language when describing salvation. Believers are repeatedly called:

- heirs of God
- joint heirs with Christ
- sons and daughters
- children of promise

These words are not metaphorical encouragement. They are juridical declarations. They are meant to establish your legal standing in the family of God, not merely stir positive emotion.

An heir does not negotiate access. An heir discovers what is already theirs.

An heir may need maturity to steward well, but they do not need permission to belong.

This is why Scripture says believers have been *"blessed with every spiritual blessing,"* not promised blessings, not potential blessings, every blessing.

"Blessed... who has blessed us with every spiritual blessing in the heavenly places in Christ" (Ephesians 1:3, NKJV).

The issue is not whether a provision exists. The issue is whether identity has caught up with reality.

Many believers live with a full inheritance but think like renters, asking for what is already theirs as though they must earn the right to ask.

Why Many Believers Live with a Scarcity Mindset

Scarcity thinking thrives where inheritance is misunderstood.

When believers see themselves primarily as servants, they expect limitation. They assume God must be convinced, appeased, or moved emotionally before He will act.

That assumption quietly turns prayer into pressure, because you begin trying to perform the "right tone" to get the "right outcome."

This produces prayers filled with anxiety:

- "What if God doesn't answer?"
- "What if I ask for too much?"
- "What if this isn't His will?"

But inheritance dissolves these fears.

A child does not hesitate to eat at the family table. They do not ask permission to drink water. They do not worry about whether provision will run out, not because resources are infinite, but because belonging is settled.

The table is not earned; it is where the family lives.

And when you know you belong, you ask differently, you wait differently, and you receive differently.

Why Faith Is the Access Point, Not the Price

Faith is often misunderstood as payment. In reality, faith is recognition.

Faith does not convince God to give. Faith agrees with what God has already given.

Faith is not you trying to move God toward generosity; it is you awakening to the generosity already revealed in Christ.

This is why Scripture consistently contrasts faith with works.

Works attempt to produce. Faith learns to receive.

Receiving does not mean passivity. It means alignment.

You align expectations with promises.

You align prayer with provision.

You align action with identity.

Receiving is active in the right direction: it stops striving to generate and begins cooperating with what has already been supplied.

This is why Jesus repeatedly responds to faith, not need.

Need recognizes lack. Faith recognizes availability.

God is not moved by desperation. He is honored by trust.

Desperation often still assumes distance. Trust assumes presence and provision.

Why Prayer Changes When Inheritance Is Understood

Prayer exposes identity more clearly than doctrine.

A servant prays, hoping. A son prays, expecting.

This does not mean sons are demanding or entitled. It means they are confident.

Confidence does not come from personality. It comes from knowing there is already access.

Confidence is not loudness. Confidence is quiet certainty that you are welcome.

When inheritance is understood:

- prayer becomes restful
- petition becomes conversation
- Thanksgiving becomes natural

You stop trying to persuade God. You start agreeing with Him.

You stop praying as though God must be convinced to care, and you begin praying from the assumption that care is already settled.

Why Delay Is Not Denial

Many believers struggle with unanswered prayer because they interpret delay as rejection.

But inheritance reframes waiting.

Delay does not question belonging. It refines trust.

An heir does not cease to be an heir because access is timed. Timing affects experience, not ownership.

Waiting is no longer a crisis when you know the account is yours. It becomes a season where faith is trained, and wisdom is formed.

This distinction preserves peace.

You can wait without anxiety when you know the account is yours.

When identity is settled, waiting becomes patience instead of panic.

Why This Threatens Performance-Based Religion

Inheritance destabilizes systems built on control.

If believers truly understand that provision flows from sonship, fear loses its leverage. Guilt loses its power. Manipulation loses effectiveness.

And when fear loses leverage, many religious systems lose their primary tool for managing people.

Religion often prefers the servant model because it produces compliance.

But God prefers the family model because it produces maturity.

He is not looking for managed servants. He is raising confident sons.

He is forming people who obey from love, not people who comply from intimidation.

From Asking "Can I?" to Knowing "I May"

One of the clearest signs that inheritance has settled is the disappearance of hesitation.

You no longer ask, "Am I allowed?" "Do I qualify?" "Is this too much?"

You know your standing.

This does not produce arrogance. It produces peaceful confidence.

And that confidence becomes the atmosphere where prayer becomes simple again, because you stop negotiating and start trusting.

A Necessary Internal Shift

You cannot live on an inheritance while thinking like an employee.

Employees measure worth by output. Heirs live from identity.

This chapter invites a shift, not in effort, but in orientation.

You are not trying to access God's generosity. You are learning to trust it.

Trust is the bridge between legal reality and lived experience.

When you trust, you stop reaching for what you already have and begin stewarding it.

Where This Leads Next

If inheritance is real and access is settled, then one question remains:

How does authority operate in the life of a believer?

Authority is not force. It is not dominance. It is not volume.

Authority flows naturally from identity and location.

That is where we go next.

Self-Reflective Questions

1. Where have you been relating to God like an employee trying to earn instead of an heir learning to receive?
2. In your prayer life, what signs show you are still negotiating rather than trusting settled access?
3. What scarcity thought tends to surface most often for you, and what would inherited truth say instead?
4. How would your obedience change if you believed it flows from belonging rather than functioning as currency?
5. Where do you need to practice faith as recognition this week, not faith as payment?

Chapter 12: Authority Flows From Identity, Not Effort

You Do Not Generate Authority; You Carry It Through Union

Authority is one of the most misunderstood concepts in Christian life. Many believers associate authority with volume, intensity, position, or spiritual exertion. Others assume authority must be requested repeatedly from God, as though it were granted temporarily based on behavior or mood.

That is why some people feel bold one day and powerless the next, even though nothing has changed in Christ. They confuse emotional energy with spiritual legitimacy.

Scripture presents something entirely different. Authority does not come from effort. It flows naturally from identity and position.

You do not exercise authority because you feel powerful. You exercise authority because you are authorized. And authorization does not come from your personality; it comes from your placement in Christ.

Why Authority Is a Matter of Legitimacy

Authority has nothing to do with force. It has everything to do with legitimacy.

A police officer does not stop traffic because of physical strength or emotional intensity. Authority resides in the badge, not in the officer's personality. Whether calm or tired, confident or uncertain, the authority remains because it is delegated.

The officer may feel weak, but the badge does not become weak. The badge represents a higher jurisdiction.

In the same way, spiritual authority does not fluctuate based on how you feel, how well you performed yesterday, or how confident you sound today.

Authority flows from union with Christ. Because Christ has authority, and you are in Christ, authority is shared, not earned.

This is why the enemy's strategy is often to attack identity first; if identity wobbles, authority becomes hesitant.

Why Jesus Never Struggled With Authority

Jesus never questioned whether demons would obey Him. He never rehearsed His identity before speaking. He never negotiated outcomes. He spoke, and things moved.

Why? Because he did not try to exercise authority. He stood in it.

Jesus understood His origin, His relationship with the Father, and His mission. Authority flowed effortlessly because identity was settled. He did not look for authority in the moment; He lived from authority as a constant reality.

Scripture now makes a staggering claim: "As He is, so are we in this world."

This does not mean believers replace Christ. It means they participate in His authority through union. Your authority is not self-created. It is derivative. It comes from sharing His life and standing, not from building your own spiritual reputation.

Why Authority Cannot Be Sustained by Fear

Fear-based authority always collapses.

When believers attempt to exercise authority from insecurity, it produces strain. They raise their voice, repeat prayers excessively, or rely on emotional intensity to compensate for uncertainty.

The strain is not proof of spiritual warfare being "stronger." It is often proof of identity that is unsettled.

Authority does not respond to anxiety. It responds to clarity.

Clarity comes from knowing:

- who you are
- where you stand
- whose authority you carry

This is why Scripture links authority to righteousness and sonship, not to effort.

When you are unsure of your standing, you will overcompensate. When your standing is settled, your words become simpler, and your actions become steadier.

Why Authority Must Be Lived Daily, Not Activated Occasionally

Many believers treat authority as a switch they flip in moments of crisis. But authority is not episodic. It is positional.

You do not activate authority; you live from it.

This is why Jesus could walk calmly into hostile environments without panic. He did not rise to authority; authority accompanied Him.

When identity is secure, authority becomes normal.

Authority is not something you borrow for emergencies; it is the posture you carry into ordinary life.

Authority without Arrogance

One of the greatest fears surrounding authoritative teaching is arrogance. But arrogance does not come from authority; it comes from self-reference.

True authority is not loud. It is not domineering. It does not need to announce itself.

Authority rooted in Christ is calm, precise, and confident, because it is not defending itself.

When you know authority is delegated, you do not have to prove anything. You simply represent what you carry.

The most authoritative people in Scripture are often the most humble, because humility flows from dependence, not weakness.

Humility is not the absence of authority; it is authority expressed without self-importance.

Why Authority Requires Submission

Authority only functions properly under submission.

Jesus repeatedly emphasized that He spoke and acted under the Father's authority. Submission did not weaken Him; it empowered Him.

In the same way, believers do not exercise authority independently. They exercise it in alignment.

Submission is not passivity. It is in agreement with divine order.

When alignment is present, authority flows freely.

Submission keeps authority pure because it keeps it connected to the Source rather than turning it into self-rule.

Why Many Believers Struggle to Exercise Authority

The problem is rarely a lack of faith. It is an unsettled identity.

When believers are unsure of their standing, they hesitate. They ask permission where none is required. They retreat where they are meant to stand.

But once identity is settled, hesitation fades.

Authority does not need to be proven. It needs to be expressed.

And expression becomes natural when you stop evaluating yourself and start standing in what Christ has already secured.

Authority and Responsibility

Authority is never given for self-promotion. It is given for representation.

Believers carry authority not to dominate, but to reflect the rule of Christ, bringing order where there is chaos, peace where there is fear, and healing where there is brokenness.

Authority is stewardship.

Stewardship means you carry authority with purpose, not for display. You carry it to serve what God is building and to push back what destroys.

A Quiet Shift That Changes Everything

When authority is understood as identity-based, everything shifts:

Prayer becomes confident.
Resistance becomes effective.
Obedience becomes responsive.
Fear loses its voice.

You stop asking, "Will this work?" You start asking, "What does alignment require here?"

That question changes your tone. It replaces panic with clarity and replaces self-effort with cooperation.

Where This Takes Us Next

Authority expressed outwardly must first be stabilized inwardly.

That requires a renewed mind, a transformation of perception, reflex, and instinct.

The Christian life is not sustained by bursts of revelation. It is sustained by transformed thinking.

That is where we go next.

Self-Reflective Questions

1. Where have you been confusing authority with emotional intensity instead of legitimacy in Christ?
2. In what situations do you tend to hesitate, and what does that hesitation reveal about your sense of standing?
3. How would your prayers change if you believed authority is carried through union and not earned through effort?
4. Where do you need to practice authority as a daily posture instead of an emergency tool?
5. What would alignment look like this week in one specific area where you want to see authority expressed?

Chapter 13: The Renewed Mind: From Revelation To Instinct

When Truth Stops Being a Lesson and Becomes Your Default Response

Revelation can change what you believe. But only a renewed mind changes how you live.

This is why you can truly believe something is right, yet still respond as if it is not real when pressure hits. Revelation can settle the message, but renewal settles the reflex.

Many believers have encountered powerful truths about identity, union, righteousness, and authority, yet still find themselves reacting to life in old patterns. Fear surfaces under pressure. Self-effort reappears in crisis. Doubt interrupts confidence.

That gap is not proof that identity is untrue. It is proof that the mind still has old pathways it defaults to when it feels unsafe.

This does not mean the revelation was false. It means revelation has not yet been integrated.

The renewed mind is where identity moves from concept to reflex.

Why Revelation Alone Is Not Enough

Revelation initiates transformation. It does not complete it.

Scripture does not say, "Be transformed by revelation." It says, *"Be transformed by the renewing of your mind"* (Romans 12:2, NKJV).

Renewal implies a process. A renewed mind is not a one-time realization. It is the gradual reprogramming of perception, learning to interpret reality from God's perspective rather than from habit, memory, or fear.

You can have a moment of insight in minutes, but it can take time for your instincts to stop reaching for the old interpretation first.

This is why believers can say "Amen" on Sunday and still panic on Monday. The mind has been informed, but not yet retrained.

How the Mind Was Originally Trained

Long before you were born again, your mind learned how to survive in a fallen world. It learned:

- self-protection
- self-promotion
- fear-based decision-making
- performance-driven worth
- emotional reasoning

These patterns were not sinful in origin. They were adaptive. They helped you cope, avoid pain, and feel in control.

The problem is that what helped you survive can now interfere with how you are meant to live as someone made new.

Once you are born again, those patterns become misaligned with your new reality.

The spirit has been made new instantly. The mind must be renewed intentionally.

That is why you can be spiritually new and still mentally familiar with fear, suspicion, and self-effort.

Renewal Is Not Positive Thinking

The renewed mind is not optimism. It is not denial. It is not repeating affirmations to override pain.

Renewal is alignment with truth.

It does not pretend that the storm is not real. It refuses to let the storm define the meaning of your life.

It is learning to ask different questions.

The unrenewed mind asks:

- "What if this goes wrong?"
- "What does this say about me?"
- "How will I survive this?"

The renewed mind asks:

- "What does God see here?"
- "How does identity respond?"
- "What does alignment look like now?"

Same situation. Different interpretation.

Renewal is not about making yourself feel better; it is about learning to think more accurately.

Why Perception Determines Reaction

You do not react to events. You react to meaning.

Two believers can face identical circumstances and respond entirely differently, not because one is stronger, but because they interpret reality differently.

The renewed mind learns to interpret from identity rather than insecurity.

It does not ignore difficulty. It reframes it.

This is why Scripture says, *"Set your mind on things above, not on things on the earth"* (Colossians 3:2, NKJV).

This is not escapism. It is perspective calibration.

Perspective calibration means you stop letting the most visible thing become the most authoritative thing.

From Conscious Effort to Automatic Response

At first, renewed thinking requires effort. You must pause. You must challenge assumptions. You must interrupt old narratives.

That interruption can feel unnatural at first, because fear-based reflexes tend to speak fast and loud.

But over time, something shifts. Truth becomes instinctive.

Just as a trained musician no longer thinks about every note, a renewed believer no longer deliberates over every response. Identity begins to respond automatically.

This is maturity.

Maturity is not perfection. It is reflex alignment.

A mature response is not the absence of emotion; it is the presence of anchored interpretation.

Why Pressure Reveals Renewal

Pressure does not create character. It reveals it.

Under pressure, you do not rise to the level of revelation; you fall to the level of renewal.

This is why God allows tension, not to punish, but to expose areas where identity has not yet been integrated.

Pressure reveals where the mind still defaults to fear instead of trust.

This is not a condemnation. It is an invitation.

When pressure exposes a fear reflex, it is showing you where the mind still needs to learn what the spirit already knows.

The Role of the Holy Spirit in Renewal

Renewal is not a solo effort.

The Holy Spirit does not merely give revelation; He facilitates renewal. He reminds, convicts, redirects, and reframes.

But he does not override the mind. He partners with it.

Renewal requires cooperation.

You choose what narratives you allow. You choose which voices you believe. You choose whether truth governs interpretation.

This is where responsibility returns, not to earn identity, but to live aligned with it.

The Spirit supplies clarity, but you still decide whether clarity becomes your new lens. Renewal Produces Rest.

As the mind renews, striving decreases.

You stop fighting to prove worth. You stop reacting defensively. You stop catastrophizing uncertainty.

Not because life becomes easier, but because identity becomes settled.

Rest is not inactivity. It is the absence of inner resistance.

Rest is what happens when your inner world stops arguing with what God has already said.

A Necessary Clarification

A renewed mind does not make you emotionless. It makes you anchored.

Feelings still arise. Thoughts still come. But they no longer dictate reality. Truth does.

Anchoring means feelings become information, not instruction.

They can be acknowledged without being obeyed.

Where This Takes Us Next

When the mind is renewed, identity no longer requires constant reinforcement. It becomes lived.

The next step is learning how this renewed identity expresses itself relationally, with God and others.

That brings us to sonship.

Self-Reflective Questions

1. Where do you most often see a gap between what you believe and how you react under pressure?
2. Which old survival pattern shows up most quickly for you: self-protection, self-effort, fear, or performance thinking?
3. What is one situation in your life right now that needs a renewed interpretation instead of an emotional reaction?
4. How do you usually respond when pressure reveals an unrenewed reflex: condemnation, denial, or invitation?
5. What practical step can you take this week to cooperate with renewal so truth becomes more instinctive in you?

Chapter 14: From Servants To Sons: The Identity That Matures

Maturity Is Measured by Relationship, Not Performance

One of the clearest indicators of spiritual maturity is how a believer relates to God.

Not how much they know.

Not how loudly they pray.

Not how disciplined they appear.

But whether they relate to God as a servant or as a son.

This is where many believers get stuck, because they may grow in knowledge while still praying, obeying, and thinking from an identity of distance.

This distinction is not semantic. It is foundational.

And until it is resolved, identity will remain unstable no matter how much revelation is received.

Why the Servant Mentality Is So Persistent

The servant mentality survives conversion easily because it feels spiritual.

Servants obey.

Servants work hard.

Servants fear disobedience.

Servants seek approval.

On the surface, these seem virtuous. But beneath them lies a subtle assumption:

"My standing is dependent on my performance."

That assumption may produce outward discipline, but it quietly produces inward anxiety, because performance can never provide lasting security.

This assumption contradicts the gospel.

Scripture does not say you were adopted because you behaved well. It says you were adopted because God chose you.

Sonship is not a reward. It is a position.

And because it is a position, it is received, not achieved.

The Difference Between Obedience and Relationship

Servants obey to avoid punishment or earn a reward. Sons obey because they belong.

The action may look the same externally, but the source is radically different.

A servant asks, "What is required of me?"

A son asks, "What reflects my Father's heart?"

Servant obedience is transactional. Sonship obedience is relational.

Transactions always keep a distance because they are based on exchange. A relationship creates closeness because it is based on belonging.

This is why Scripture says:

"You did not receive the spirit of bondage again to fear, but you received the Spirit of adoption" (Romans 8:15, NKJV).

Fear signals servant thinking. Confidence signals sonship.

Why Fear Is the Default Language of Servanthood

Fear governs servants because servants lack security.

They fear:

- losing favor
- failing expectations
- disappointing authority
- being replaced

This fear quietly shapes prayer, worship, and decision-making.

Servant prayer is cautious.

Servant worship is performance-aware.

Servant faith is conditional.

But sons do not fear abandonment. They live from belonging.

Belonging does not remove reverence, but it removes dread. It replaces the fear of rejection with the confidence of being held.

Why Sonship Does Not Eliminate Discipline

Sonship does not mean indulgence. It means security under correction.

A servant interprets correction as rejection. A son interprets correction as investment.

Discipline does not threaten identity. It confirms the relationship.

This is why Scripture says God disciplines those He loves, not those He tolerates.

Discipline is not God distancing Himself from you. It is God drawing you into maturity because you matter to Him.

The Cost of Remaining a Servant

Many believers remain spiritually immature not because they lack revelation, but because they resist sonship.

Sonship requires surrendering control. Servanthood preserves self-effort.

As long as you are a servant, you remain the engine. As a son, you become the vessel.

That is a painful shift for the religious mind, because self-effort feels safer than surrender.

But self-effort eventually produces exhaustion, because it asks you to carry what only grace can carry.

This is why many believers burn out. They are faithful servants carrying weights they were never meant to carry.

God did not call you to manage your own transformation. He called you to abide.

Abiding means you stop trying to produce life and instead remain connected to the Source of life.

Why Sonship Changes Prayer Completely

Prayer exposes identity more than theology.

Servants pray to be heard. Sons pray because they are heard.

This does not produce arrogance. It produces rest.

Sons do not measure prayer by intensity. They measure it by alignment.

They are not afraid of silence. They are not anxious about outcomes.

They have a trust relationship.

They do not treat prayer as a performance review. They treat prayer as communion with the One who already calls them His own.

Why Sonship Produces Authority Without Strain

Servants can be delegated tasks. Only sons carry authority.

Authority flows from belonging, not effort.

This is why Jesus repeatedly emphasized His relationship with the Father. He did not assert authority by volume or force. He stood in identity.

Believers who live as sons do not struggle to exercise authority. They do not need to prove anything.

They simply represent.

Representation is what sons do. They carry the Father's name, reflect the Father's heart, and move with the Father's confidence.

Why Sonship Is the Goal of Redemption

Salvation was never about creating obedient workers. It was about restoring family.

God did not send His Son to recruit servants. He sent His Son to bring many sons to glory.

Everything in redemption, justification, reconciliation, indwelling, and inheritance points toward sonship.

If your Christianity does not move you toward sonship, it has stalled.

A stalled Christianity often looks busy, but it feels anxious because the engine is still self-effort instead of belonging.

A Necessary Internal Question

At this point, the question is unavoidable:

Do you obey God primarily because you fear consequences, or because you know you belong?

Your answer will shape everything that follows.

And your answer will also explain your prayer life, because the way you approach God reveals the identity you believe you have.

Where This Takes Us Next

When sonship is settled, one more transformation occurs:

Prayer stops sounding like begging. It becomes a partnership.

That shift must be addressed carefully, because it reshapes how believers relate to God's will, timing, and action.

Self-Reflective Questions

1. Where do you relate to God more like a servant than a son, and how can you tell?
2. What fear shows up most often in your spiritual life, and what does it reveal about your sense of belonging?
3. How do you usually interpret correction from God: rejection, disappointment, or investment?
4. When you pray, do you pray like you are trying to be heard, or like you already are heard?
5. What would change this week if you consciously obeyed from belonging instead of from fear?

Chapter 15: Prayer Without Begging: Confidence Rooted In Identity

Prayer Is Not a Plea for Access; It Is the Expression of Belonging

Nothing exposes how a believer sees themselves more clearly than the way they pray.

Prayer reveals identity before it reveals theology. You can say all the right doctrines, but your prayer posture will reveal what you truly believe about access, acceptance, and God's disposition toward you.

Many prayers sound sincere, passionate, even desperate, yet are quietly shaped by insecurity.

They are filled with repetition, apology, pleading, and fear of rejection. God is approached cautiously, as though access were fragile and favor uncertain.

That cautious approach usually has a history behind it: disappointment, fear, performance conditioning, or a misunderstanding of sonship.

This posture is not humility. It is an unresolved identity.

Why Begging Prayer Feels Spiritual, but Isn't

Begging feels spiritual because it sounds earnest. It carries emotional weight. It communicates dependence.

But it also communicates something else: distance.

It suggests that God is reluctant, that access is fragile, and that the relationship is still being negotiated.

Begging assumes:

- Access is uncertain
- Favor is conditional
- God must be persuaded
- The answer depends on intensity

None of these assumptions survives the New Covenant.

Begging prayer often sounds like dependence, but underneath it can be an attempt to control outcomes through emotion, as if enough intensity can guarantee a response.

Scripture does not invite believers to beg. It invites them to draw near with confidence.

"Let us therefore come boldly to the throne of grace" (Hebrews 4:16, NKJV).

Confidence is not arrogance. It is in agreement with reality.

How Jesus Prayed, and Why It Matters

Jesus never begged the Father. He asked. He declared. He gave thanks.

Even before miracles occurred, He thanked the Father, not because outcomes were visible, but because the relationship was secure.

Thanksgiving in advance is not presumption; it is relational certainty. It is what happens when the bond is settled, and the heart is at rest.

This matters because Scripture declares that believers now share His relationship with the Father.

You are not trying to earn the right to pray like Jesus. You are learning to pray from the relationship Jesus has already opened.

If your prayer posture does not reflect sonship, something is misaligned.

Why Begging Undermines Faith

Begging subtly contradicts faith.

Faith says, "I trust what You have said."
Begging says, "I'm not sure you will."

Faith rests in promise. Begging reacts to fear.

Fear may be understandable, but it cannot be your governor, because fear interprets God through uncertainty instead of through covenant.

This does not mean believers should suppress emotion. It means emotion should not define posture.

You can be desperate and confident at the same time, but confidence must govern.

Desperation describes the need. Confidence describes the relationship.

One can be intense, but the other must be stable.

Why Prayer Is Not Persuasion

God does not need to be convinced to be good. He does not need to be reminded to be faithful. He does not need emotional leverage to act.

Prayer is not about changing God's mind. It is about aligning with God's will.

Prayer is not you trying to pull heaven toward your agenda; it is you learning to participate in what heaven is already doing.

This is why Scripture says:

"If we ask according to His will, we know that we have what we ask."

Notice the language: *have*, not hope to have.

Prayer is not lobbying heaven. It is participating in what heaven has already decided.

This is why alignment matters more than intensity, because alignment produces confidence that does not rise and fall with mood.

The Role of Asking in Sonship

Asking does not contradict confidence. It expresses a relationship.

A child asks freely, not because they doubt love, but because they trust it.

Asking in sonship sounds different:

- It is direct

- It is honest
- It is expectant
- It is peaceful

There is no performance. No theatrics. No fear of asking incorrectly.

Sonship prayer is not scripted to impress. It is spoken to relate.

It is less about sounding spiritual and more about being sincere and aligned.

Why Thanksgiving Is the Language of Confidence

Thanksgiving is the clearest evidence of faith.

You do not thank someone for something you doubt they will give.

This is why Scripture often pairs prayer with thanksgiving, not as a courtesy, but as evidence of trust.

Thanksgiving says, "I trust You enough to rest."

It also protects your heart from panic, because thanksgiving shifts your attention from what is missing to what is certain: the faithfulness of God.

When Silence Does Not Mean Absence

Many believers panic in silence.

When answers are delayed, they assume distance. When emotions go quiet, they assume God has withdrawn.

But silence does not negate presence.

A son does not panic when the Father is quiet. He trusts the relationship.

Silence often deepens trust more than answers ever could.

Silence is not always a closed door. Sometimes it is God training you to rest in who He is rather than in what you feel.

From Prayer as Survival to Prayer as Communion

Begging prayer is survival-oriented. Sonship prayer is relational.

One is driven by fear of lack. The other by confidence of presence.

Prayer was never meant to be a crisis hotline. It was meant to be communion.

Requests emerge naturally from a relationship, not desperation.

Communion produces clarity. Desperation often produces noise.

When communion becomes the foundation, requests become simpler, and trust becomes steadier.

Why This Shift Changes Everything

When prayer is freed from begging:

- anxiety diminishes
- faith stabilizes
- confidence increases
- authority flows naturally

You stop asking, "Did I pray hard enough?" You start asking, "Am I aligned?"

That question produces peace.

And peace does not weaken prayer; it strengthens it, because it keeps you rooted in a relationship rather than tossed by fear.

A Necessary Invitation

This chapter invites you to lay down a posture, not prayer itself.

You are not being asked to pray less. You are being invited to pray from who you are.

You do not approach God as a distant deity. You approach Him as Father.

And when you approach as Father, you stop bracing for rejection and start expecting the relationship to carry you through the process.

Where This Takes Us Next

When prayer shifts, something else shifts quietly but profoundly:

Dependence stops feeling like weakness and becomes strength.

That paradox must be addressed carefully, because it reshapes how believers understand power, weakness, and maturity.

Self-Reflective Questions

1. What does your prayer posture reveal about how you see God, as a Father or a distant authority?
2. Where do you tend to beg, repeat, or apologize excessively in prayer, and what fear is beneath that pattern?
3. How would your prayers change if you believed access is settled and favor is anchored in Christ?
4. What role does thanksgiving currently play in your prayer life, and what would it look like to practice it as trust?
5. When God feels silent, do you interpret it as absence, delay, or an invitation to deeper trust, and why?

Chapter 16: Dependence As Strength: The Paradox Of Maturity

The Deeper You Grow, The More You Rely

One of the most deeply ingrained assumptions in human thinking is that maturity equals independence.

From childhood onward, growth is measured by how little help is needed. Strength is associated with self-sufficiency. Dependence is equated with weakness.

That mindset makes sense in natural development, but it becomes dangerous when it becomes your spiritual blueprint, because it trains you to "outgrow" the very dependence the Kingdom was designed to deepen.

But the Kingdom of God reverses this logic completely.

In Christ, maturity does not lead to independence from God. It leads to deeper dependence.

The goal is not that you need God less; the goal is that you trust Him more fully and rely on Him more naturally.

This paradox unsettles the self-reliant mind, but it is the only path to sustainable spiritual life.

Why Self-Sufficiency Is The Enemy Of Union

Self-sufficiency thrives on control.

It says, "I've got this."

"I can manage."

"I'll ask for help if I fail."

It sounds responsible, but it quietly keeps you at the center, because you remain the one determining when you will allow God to participate.

But the union dismantles this posture.

Union says, "I cannot live this life apart from Him, and I was never meant to."

This is not a resignation. It is designed.

Union is not God assisting your agenda; union is God becoming your life.

The Christian life is not difficult to live independently; it is impossible.

This is why Christ does not assist your independent life. He replaces it with His own.

If you try to live the new life with the old engine, you will experience constant strain, because self-effort cannot carry what only Christ can sustain.

Paul's Confession Of Strength Through Weakness

Paul's declaration, "When I am weak, then I am strong", is often quoted but rarely understood.

Paul was not celebrating failure. He was celebrating clarity.

Weakness exposes the limits of self-effort. It reveals the boundary beyond which human strength cannot go.

And at that boundary, something else becomes available: grace.

Grace begins where self-sufficiency ends, not because God is withholding, but because self-reliance blocks the flow of dependence.

Grace is not God helping you do better. Grace is God doing through you what you cannot do yourself.

This is why Paul says:

"My grace is sufficient for you, for My power is made perfect in weakness" (2 Corinthians 12:9, NKJV).

Power does not wait for strength. It flows where dependence exists.

Weakness becomes a doorway when it turns you toward Christ instead of inward toward self-analysis.

Why Dependence Is Not Passivity

Dependence is often confused with inactivity. But dependence is not doing nothing; it is doing nothing alone.

A dependent believer still acts, still decides, and still obeys, but from a posture of reliance rather than control.

Dependence does not remove responsibility; it removes isolation.

It means you stop making decisions as if you are the only one involved.

Self-effort says, "Let me try harder."

Dependence says, "Christ, live this through me."

That prayer does not weaken action. It purifies it.

It strips away frantic striving and replaces it with cooperation, so your effort becomes responsive instead of pressured.

Why Independence Produces Burnout

Many believers burn out not because they are unfaithful, but because they are self-reliant.

They carry responsibilities God never asked them to carry alone.

They manage emotions God intended to heal.

They shoulder outcomes God intended to direct.

They live as if everything depends on them, and then call the strain "dedication," when it is often just independence wearing spiritual language.

This produces exhaustion disguised as dedication.

But Christ never invited believers to carry the Christian life. He invited them to abide.

Abiding is not laziness. It is a sustained connection.

Abiding means you stay connected to the Source instead of trying to function on stored strength.

It is a daily posture, not a crisis tool.

Why Dependence Produces Authority

This may seem counterintuitive, but the most authoritative believers are often the most dependent.

Authority does not come from personal strength. It comes from alignment with Christ's life.

Jesus exercised authority effortlessly because He lived in constant dependence on the Father.

He did nothing independently, not because He lacked power, but because the union was His source.

Dependence did not make Him weak; it made Him precise.

It kept His words clean, His actions aligned, and His authority uncompromised.

Believers walk in authority not by asserting themselves, but by yielding.

Yielding does not mean shrinking back. It means stepping forward while remaining connected.

The End Of Self-Confidence

This chapter requires the surrender of a subtle idol: self-confidence.

Self-confidence trusts the self. Kingdom confidence trusts Christ within.

This does not diminish courage. It redirects it.

Courage rooted in self collapses under pressure. Courage rooted in Christ remains steady.

Self-confidence has to keep proving itself. Kingdom confidence rests because it is anchored in Someone who does not fluctuate.

Why Dependence Produces Peace

Peace is not the absence of challenge. It is the absence of inner resistance.

When you stop trying to carry what was never meant to be carried, peace emerges naturally.

You no longer ask, "Can I handle this?" You ask, "How is Christ expressing Himself here?"

That shift transforms stress into expectancy.

Peace does not mean you stop caring. It means you stop controlling.

It means you remain engaged without being internally crushed.

A Necessary Reframing Of Maturity

Spiritual maturity is not about becoming more capable on your own. It is becoming more aware of your need for Him.

The most mature believers are not those who pray the least. They are those who depend the most deeply.

Maturity does not remove dependence; it refines it.

It turns dependence from emergency language into daily language.

Where This Takes Us Next

When dependence becomes strength, another transformation follows:

Boldness without arrogance.

This boldness is not loud, not self-promoting, and not defensive. It flows quietly from identity and union.

That balance must be explored carefully.

Self-Reflective Questions

1. Where do you still measure maturity by independence instead of deeper dependence on Christ?
2. What situation in your life right now reveals self-sufficiency most clearly, and what would it look like to yield instead?
3. When you feel weak, do you tend to withdraw, strive harder, or let weakness become clarity that leads you to grace?
4. In what area have you been carrying responsibility alone that you were meant to carry in abiding dependence?
5. What would change this week if you replaced "Let me try harder" with "Christ, live this through me" in one specific area?

Chapter 17: Boldness Without Arrogance: Confidence Rooted In Union

When Identity Is Settled, Courage Becomes Quiet and Clean

Boldness is often misunderstood and frequently avoided because it is confused with arrogance.

Many believers have seen confidence expressed as domination, loudness, self-promotion, or spiritual intimidation. As a result, they retreat into passivity, mistaking timidity for humility.

That retreat can feel safe, but it quietly limits love, limits obedience, and limits authority, because it makes fear look like wisdom.

But Scripture presents a different picture entirely.

Boldness is not self-assertion. Boldness is identity clarity.

When identity is settled, boldness becomes natural, and arrogance unnecessary.

You stop trying to look strong, and you start living from what is true. That change removes both the need to perform and the need to hide.

Why Arrogance Is a Sign of Insecurity

Arrogance always points inward.

It is loud because it is uncertain.

It dominates because it is threatened.

It boasts because it needs validation.

Arrogance arises when a person must prove who they are.

Boldness, by contrast, does not need to announce itself. It stands quietly because it is secure.

Arrogance is identity fighting for space. Boldness is identity resting in place.

This is why Jesus could remain silent before accusations and calm before hostility. He did not need to defend His identity, it was already settled.

When identity is settled, you can let noise stay noise, because you are not living for approval.

The Difference Between Self-Confidence and Christ-Confidence

Self-confidence draws from personal ability. Christ-confidence draws from union.

Self-confidence asks, "Am I capable?"

Christ-confidence asks, "Is Christ present?"

One fluctuates. The other remains.

This is why Scripture never exhorts believers to believe in themselves. It consistently calls them to trust Christ within.

Self-confidence rises and falls with performance. Christ-confidence remains steady because it is anchored in relationship and indwelling.

Confidence rooted in Christ does not inflate the ego. It anchors the soul.

It does not make you bigger than others; it makes you steadier than your circumstances.

Why Humility and Boldness Are Not Opposites

Religion often presents humility and boldness as opposites, implying that to be humble, one must be hesitant, apologetic, or unsure.

But humility is not self-diminishment. Humility is accurate self-perception.

A humble believer agrees with God about who they are and who God is.

This produces a paradox:

- humility without insecurity
- boldness without pride
- authority without domination

Jesus embodied this perfectly. He washed feet without losing authority. He confronted hypocrisy without anger. He spoke truth without fear.

True humility does not erase identity; it removes self-importance.

That is why boldness can remain clean, because it is not trying to elevate the self.

Why Boldness Emerges From Sonship

Servants hesitate because they fear rejection. Sons act because they know they belong.

Boldness flows naturally from sonship because there is nothing left to earn and nothing left to prove.

This is why Scripture repeatedly associates boldness with access:

"We have confidence to enter…"

Confidence is not personality-driven. It is relationship-driven.

Access produces boldness because access means you are not approaching as a stranger; you are approaching as family.

Why Boldness Is Often Quiet

True boldness does not require volume.

It does not need to dominate conversations, control outcomes, or intimidate opposition.

It simply stands.

This quiet strength unsettles those accustomed to performance-based authority.

Boldness rooted in union is calm under pressure, clear in decision, and steady in adversity.

It does not react. It responds.

Reaction is often fear, trying to protect identity. Response is identity acting from rest.

Why Boldness Requires Rest

Rest is the hidden engine of boldness.

Striving believers hesitate because they are already exhausted. They fear confrontation because they fear failure. They avoid responsibility because they fear exposure.

But rest removes fear.

When you are no longer trying to protect identity, you can speak freely. When you are no longer striving to maintain standing, you can act decisively.

Boldness without rest collapses into arrogance.

Rest without boldness collapses into passivity.

Identity produces both.

Rest produces the inner quiet that keeps boldness from becoming harsh, and boldness produces the courage that keeps rest from becoming avoidance.

Why Boldness Is Necessary for Love

Love without boldness becomes accommodation. Boldness without love becomes aggression.

Christlike love requires courage.

Jesus did not avoid hard conversations. He did not confuse kindness with silence.

He spoke truth because He loved, and He loved without fear because identity was settled.

Believers who avoid boldness in the name of love often end up withholding what is most needed.

Love that refuses courage often protects comfort more than it protects people.

From Reaction to Representation

Boldness rooted in union shifts behavior from reaction to representation.

You stop reacting to offense.

You stop defending yourself.

You stop striving to be understood.

You begin representing Christ.

Representation does not require dominance. It requires presence.

When you represent Christ, you no longer need to win arguments to protect your worth.

You can speak truth, keep love, and remain steady.

A Necessary Checkpoint

At this stage of the journey, a quiet question emerges:

Do you avoid boldness because you fear pride, or because identity is still unsettled?

True humility does not hide. It stands accurately.

Avoidance can look like humility, but it often exposes fear.

Accuracy is the test: are you agreeing with God, or are you shrinking back from what He has said?

Where This Takes Us Next

When boldness is settled, identity becomes normal rather than exceptional.

The final transformation occurs when identity no longer feels like something to maintain, but something that simply is.

That is where the journey concludes.

Self-Reflective Questions

1. Where have you avoided boldness because you feared being seen as arrogant, and what was the cost of that avoidance?
2. In what situations do you notice self-confidence fluctuating, and what would it look like to practice Christ-confidence instead?
3. Do you tend to react under pressure or respond from rest, and what does that reveal about your sense of identity?
4. Where do you need to show boldness as an act of love rather than staying silent for comfort?
5. Do you avoid boldness because you fear pride, or because you are still unsure you belong, and how can sonship settle that?

Chapter 18: When Identity Becomes Normal

The End of Performing Spiritual Life and the Beginning of Living From Union

The goal of the Christian life is not a heightened spiritual state. It is normalcy.

Not ordinary in the sense of powerlessness, but normal in the sense of unforced, integrated, and lived from within.

Normalcy is where truth stops being something you reach for in emergencies and becomes the quiet atmosphere of how you think, respond, and walk through life.

When identity is still fragile, believers experience spiritual life as something they must remember, rehearse, or reassert.

They "get into faith," "step into authority," or "try to walk in love." These phrases are not wrong; they often describe early growth. But they also reveal that identity still feels like a place you enter instead of a place you inhabit.

Maturity looks different.

Maturity is when identity no longer feels like something you visit. It becomes the place you live in.

Why Normalcy Is the Final Mark of Maturity

Anything that requires constant maintenance is not yet integrated.

At first, revelation must be consciously recalled:

"I am righteous."

"I am in Christ."

"Christ lives in me."

But over time, repetition gives way to reflex.

You no longer remind yourself who you are in every situation. You respond as who you are.

This is not forgetting truth; it is truth becoming instinctive.

It moves from being a statement you repeat to a lens you naturally see through.

This is when righteousness feels natural, not heroic.

When faith feels steady, not strained.

When peace interrupts panic instinctively.

Identity has become normal.

Normal does not mean shallow; it means settled. It means the foundation is no longer shaken every time circumstances shift.

Why Many Believers Live in Peaks and Valleys

Spiritual peaks and valleys are often signs of unresolved integration.

Revelation produces peaks. Pressure reveals valleys.

Believers soar after encounters, teachings, and conferences, but struggle when routine returns.

This is not failure. It is an unfinished renewal.

A peak is not a problem, but if you require peaks to stay stable, then identity is still being supported by intensity rather than integration.

God does not desire believers who need constant stimulation. He desires believers who live anchored.

Normal identity does not require constant intensity. It sustains consistency.

Consistency is not boring; it is maturity. It is faith that remains steady when nothing feels dramatic

Life Lived From the Inside Out

When identity is settled:

- obedience flows rather than strains
- love expresses itself without calculation
- prayer becomes conversation
- authority becomes quiet confidence

Life is no longer lived *for* God. It is lived *from* God.

This is the essence of union.

Living for God can still carry hidden pressure if the engine is self-effort. Living from God means the Source is inside, and obedience becomes a response rather than a performance.

You stop asking, "What would Jesus do?" and start recognizing, "Christ is living through me."

That shift changes everything.

You do not lose responsibility in that shift; you gain clarity.

You stop guessing what holiness should look like and begin yielding to the One who is holy within you.

Why Failure No Longer Defines the Story

Normal identity does not eliminate mistakes. It eliminates identity collapse.

When failure occurs, the unrenewed mind spirals:

"What does this say about me?"

But settled identity asks a different question:

"What alignment is needed here?"

Failure becomes informational, not condemnatory. Correction becomes directional, not punitive.

This is freedom.

Freedom is not failing. Freedom is failing without being dragged back into an old identity story.

Why This Produces Stability in a Chaotic World

The world is unstable by nature. Circumstances fluctuate. Systems fail. People disappoint.

If identity is built on externals, instability is inevitable.

But when identity is anchored in Christ:

- Chaos loses authority
- Fear loses narrative control
- Uncertainty loses intimidation

This does not make believers detached. It makes them grounded.

Grounded people become anchors for others.

A grounded believer does not deny chaos; they refuse to let chaos interpret reality.

They bring steadiness into rooms where everyone else is reacting.

Why This Is the Goal of Discipleship

Discipleship is not information transfer. It is identity formation.

Jesus did not spend three years giving His disciples techniques. He formed perspective, relationship, and trust, so that after His departure, they could live in union.

The goal was never dependence on His physical presence. It was the embodiment of His life.

That same goal remains today.

Discipleship is successful when you stop needing constant reminders to belong and begin living as someone who knows you do.

A Final Clarification

This book has not attempted to make you:

- more impressive
- more mystical
- or more elite

It has aimed to make you accurate.

Accurate about:

- who you are
- where you stand
- and how you live

Accuracy produces peace.

Because when truth is clear, you stop negotiating identity, stop rehearsing insecurity, and stop living as though the covenant is fragile.

You live steadily, and that steadiness becomes a witness all by itself.

Self-Reflective Questions

1. Where does your spiritual life still feel like something you "enter" instead of something you live from?
2. What situation most often triggers a peak-and-valley cycle for you, and what does that reveal about integration?
3. When you fail, do you tend to collapse into identity questions or move toward alignment questions, and why?
4. What would "life lived from God" look like in one ordinary part of your daily routine this week?
5. What one truth from this book needs to move from rehearsal to reflex in your life right now?

Final Conclusion

Who Do You Think You Are?

That question has echoed since the beginning.

The serpent asked it with accusation:
"Did God really say…?"

Religion asks it with insecurity:
"Who do you think you are to expect this?"

But heaven asks it with expectation.

Who do you think you are?

If you answer from memory, fear, or performance, life will remain reactive.
But if you answer from revelation:

- I am in Christ.
- Christ lives in me.
- I am righteous by gift.
- I am a son, not a servant.
- I live from inheritance, not effort.
- I walk in authority without striving.
- I depend on Him without weakness.
- I stand without arrogance.

Then life changes, not because circumstances disappear, but because identity is settled.

You stop trying to become. You start learning how to live from what already is.

This is not an arrival. It is alignment.
Not striving upward, but resting inward.

And from that place, Christ lives His life through you, quietly, powerfully, consistently.

A Final Declaration

I am not defined by my past.

I am not governed by my feelings.

I am not limited by my failures.

I am who God says I am.

I am in Christ.

Christ lives in me.

I live from identity, not effort.

From union, not imitation.

From inheritance, not fear.

And I allow Christ to express His life through me, today, tomorrow, and continually.